Praise for *Breaking*

"A must-read for anyone who is struggling in their relationships . . . and for the narcissist in all of us."

—Dr. Abraham J. Twerski, renowned psychiatrist, pioneer
in the field of addiction, and author of over 80 books

"This book brings to the field a higher caliber effort in assisting both mental health professionals and the public to achieve a deeper understanding of narcissism and a unique approach to overcoming its deleterious effects on relationships. 'Dr G's' personal warmth and original clinical style comes through clearly in this book, and engages the reader to work towards achieving a higher level of being. Dr G is an exceptional psychologist, and I have personally known him and have collaborated with him professionally for over 20 years. This book is an excellent representation of his dedication to his patients, his passion for understanding the human mind and soul, and his drive to help people be the best that they can be. I can't recommend it enough."

—Dr. Silvina Belmonte, popular Miami psychotherapist, clinical
sexologist, and TV personality on Telemundo and Univision

"*Breaking the Mirror* is an exceptionally intelligent and accessible book on the subject of narcissism by a clinician who has had wide experience over 30 years working with people struggling with this problem. This is a wise and entertaining narrative, filled with engaging clinical case studies and innovative examples of how to deal with narcissism, both in oneself and the people we deal with in our lives. This book should become a classic, right up there with *Trapped in the Mirror* and *Disarming the Narcissist*. Highly recommended!

—Roberta Shapiro, M.Ed, LCSW, NBCCH,
Noted psychotherapist and author

BREAKING
THE
MIRROR–
OVERCOMING
NARCISSISM

How to Conquer Self-Centeredness
and Achieve Successful Relationships

Norman Goldwasser, Ph.D.

Published by
Horizon Psychology Services
MIAMI BEACH, FLORIDA

The purpose of this book is to educate. It is not intended to serve as a replacement for professional medical advice. Any use of the information in this book is at the reader's discretion. This book is sold with the understanding that neither the publisher nor the author have any liability or responsibility for any injury caused or alleged to be caused directly or indirectly by the information contained in this book. While every effort has been made to ensure its accuracy, the book's contents should not be construed as medical advice. To obtain medical advice on your individual health needs, please consult a qualified health care practitioner.

ISBN: Print: 978-0-578-90324-8
        Ebook: 978-0-578-90325-5

Cover and Interior: Gary A. Rosenberg • www.thebookcouple.com
Editing: Erica Rauzin

Printed in the United States of America

Contents

INTRODUCTION

The Reason for This Book

Almost 40 years ago, I saw my first patient at a Student Services clinic at Virginia Commonwealth University, where I had begun working toward a PhD in Clinical Psychology a year earlier. You never forget your first girlfriend, and you also never forget your first patient.

An affable, obese man in his 30s, Lee [*The case histories in this book are real but all the names are changed to protect patient confidentiality*] had never experienced a significant successful relationship because, as he said, "Women just can't handle my intense sensuality." It was my first entry into the complex world of narcissism. I also will never forget what my practicum supervisor told me when I first presented the case: "What a way to start a career in therapy—you've got yourself a real doozy." Lee was definitely a challenge, as the web that he had woven to protect his precariously fragile ego allowed him to delude himself into believing that he was too superior for any woman, instead of the deflating reality that women actually found him shallow, self-aggrandizing, and physically unappealing.

The truth is that I owe Lee a great deal, since the nine months of work that we did together taught me volumes about how the defense mechanisms involved in narcissism operate. I saw firsthand how his layers of defenses, self-absorption, and his inability to see beyond his own perspective derailed his ability to function in a genuine relationship, which only perpetuated the underlying dynamic of inadequacy and worthlessness.

Week after week, we arduously worked to unravel the complexities of his personality, and to help him to uncover the real Lee.

At a sudden point of clarity, he had an epiphany and described his real self as a "shriveled up prune—empty and pathetic." At that point of painful self-awareness, he began to cry uncontrollably, which, although excruciating, ended up being the therapeutic breakthrough he needed to get beyond the narcissistic delusions that he had built up to deflect the insecurity and inadequacy that had plagued him since childhood. The real healing could begin only once he was able to get in touch with his inner self. Only then could he be more anchored in reality in terms of what had happened to damage him and render him so ineffective in his relationships. The combination of an abusive, neglectful father and an alcoholic, self-indulgent mother resulted in a child who, at some level, realized that if he was going to get any of his needs met, he would have to focus on himself and to endlessly feed himself, both literally and figuratively.

Working with Lee as a spanking new practicum student was akin to a new recruit being sent to the front lines after a week of basic training. At first, I felt like a deer staring at headlights, but steadily over time, and with much guidance and support, as well as a good dose of challenging feedback from an extraordinarily gifted clinical supervisor, Dr. Donald Kiesler, I was able to develop my clinical skills. At the same time, I was also able to help Lee to step into reality, understand the negative impact he was having on others, begin the painful task of repairing his dysfunctional personality, and eventually heal his soul. Little did I know that my work with Lee would help prepare me for what has now become well over three decades of working with men and women who have struggled with the ravages of damaging (and damaged) parents who lacked in themselves the inner resources that are necessary to nurture a developing child.

The concept behind this book was stored in the hard drive of my mind for more than ten years, before I actually found the time and the commitment to sit down and begin to write it. It emerged from the realization that, as opposed to the countless number of self-help books that are available about everything from depression to codependency to ADHD and everywhere else across the spectrum of psychological maladies, there was literally nothing to help someone recover from the many varied challenges of narcissism.

As a strong advocate of bibliotherapy—the practice of referring patients to read good books that can be extremely helpful adjuncts to therapy—I routinely recommend, if not require, that patients read books that can provide needed compensatory information and skills to help them achieve their therapeutic goals. In fact, for years, my idea of a fun Saturday night date with my late wife was to go to the closest Barnes and Noble and scan the shelves of the Psychology and Self-Help sections to see what I could find to add to the selection of books in my office. I would look specifically for books I could offer particular patients to help them better understand themselves and, more importantly, accomplish their therapeutic goals. (Fortunately, my wife had the same passion for books and the same concept of a good date.)

However, it became apparent over time that, although the bookstore offers many books on narcissism, all of them, without exception, focused on understanding, explaining, or analyzing various aspects of the disorder, mostly from a psychoanalytic, psychodynamic, or family systems perspective. Those are important, but not sufficient. Experts wrote many of them to help poor, unsuspecting spouses identify the narcissism in their partners or learn how to run like hell to escape from the torture of a relationship with a narcissist. To my surprise and disappointment, however, I could not find a single book that was specifically designed to help individuals with narcissistic personalities overcome the challenges of this pernicious disorder and to assist them in achieving successful relationships, healthy self-love, and inner peace.

That is the impetus behind this book. My goal is to facilitate a deeper understanding of how the narcissistic personality develops and to offer real solutions for healing the emotional wounds underlying the disorder. This book strives to lay out, in a systematic and, I hope, user-friendly format, a plan to help transform the reader into a healthy, other-centered person with the insight and skills that are prerequisites to achieving effective, meaningful relationships.

Section I reviews the concept of narcissism, potential causes of the condition, diagnostic considerations, ways of measuring its impact, and descriptive parameters. It also covers issues involving co-morbidity or coexisting disorders that are often associated with narcissism, as well as common defense mechanisms that are often a part of the narcissistic dynamic.

Section II covers the different effects that narcissism has on individuals and the various ways that narcissism manifests in different people. Chapters in this section deal with cognitive processing difficulties, perceptual distortions, and emotional effects, as well as how narcissism affects relationships, achievement, and spirituality.

Section III involves the different aspects of treatment that are essential in assisting individuals affected by narcissism. It outlines the therapeutic approaches that can help them to gain more insight and understanding into their personalities and to improve their emotional and interpersonal functioning. Its chapters deal with the challenges that individuals face within the therapy process and the common goals patients often work on in therapy. It covers specific psychotherapeutic modalities often used to treat personality disorders, especially involving narcissism. One chapter focuses on a unique therapy group for men who came from narcissistic families and who have been struggling with this aspect of their personalities and the effects on their relationships. This group has been ongoing for more than 20 years, and many of the insights and tools in this book originated from that extraordinarily brave and special group of men.

Section IV is written specifically for readers who are dealing with narcissistic people—spouses, parents, children, siblings, partners, co-workers, and others. The section gives them the understanding and tools they need to be effective in building and maintaining successful relationships with these challenging people. Chapters in this section deal with the need for mindful awareness to allow for optimal functioning in these relationships, the value of strategizing, and the usefulness of rational versus emotional thinking. The section stresses the importance of preserving one's personal integrity and dignity while dealing with people who are critical and judgmental, the hallmark of narcissism. One chapter underscores the critical importance of effective communication to balance assertion and validation and to resolve conflicts. Using these conflict resolution skills can promote collaborative communication and improve readers' ability to resolve conflicts that may derail relationship stability. Finally, the section ends with the caveat that it is essential to remember that, although you must always look honestly at any contribution you may be making to the problems in a relationship, the bottom line here is that these issues are mostly not about you, but rather about the person with narcissism. The disorder is at the root of the relationship problem.

The final section, Section V, contains testimonials that patients wrote in their own words explaining how narcissism had affected them and their relationships, and how they overcame these lifelong personality problems. These stories are profound and powerful. They represent the hope of real change for those who are dealing with these challenges, a hope that readers can hold on to in their own journeys of healing and recovery. The people who wrote these testimonials are heroes in my eyes. To this day, they still help give me the motivation and strength to continue to do this often arduous and challenging work. They have allowed me to focus on the fact that people can really change who they are, how they behave, and how they think, in the process of becoming the mature, effective, and successful people that they ultimately wish to become.

Finally, I wish to dedicate this book to my late wife, Janet (also called, in Hebrew, Zahava), who was taken away from us far too early. Her support and encouragement enabled me to become the clinician, and the person, that I have become. The wisdom, inspiration, and partnership that she provided assisted me to achieve all that I have accomplished. She will be forever missed by all who knew and loved her. Also, my gratitude goes to my late, deeply beloved parents Eli and Miriam, the heroes of my life, who survived the unspeakable horrors of the Holocaust, and gave me the love, support, and normalcy to help me to realize my dreams. I am also grateful to my seven children, who are living lives that make me enormously proud, and to my 23 amazingly beautiful and loving grandchildren, who are, and always will be, the lights of my life.

I would also like to thank my dear neighbor and friend, Erica Rauzin, who did a superb job of editing and being supportive of the entire process.

She and her husband, Alan, have also been a lifeline for me—in the best of times and also in the worst of times. I also would like to thank Gary Rosenberg of The Book Couple for being so pleasant and adept in helping to get this published and into the light of day, and also Charlotte Kendrick in the U.K., who did a masterful job of proofreading the draft and helped to get it to its final stage of completion.

I also want to thank my beloved in-law Rabbi Nochum Stilerman, who inspired me to continue to work on this project when I had lost my way. He will always have my love and appreciation. And, most importantly, my deepest love and gratitude goes to my wonderful wife, Karen, who has been instrumental in my renewal and has given me the hope that a shattered life can be rebuilt. She is the ultimate partner who fills my life with joy and lightness, and she has inspired me to (finally) get this done.

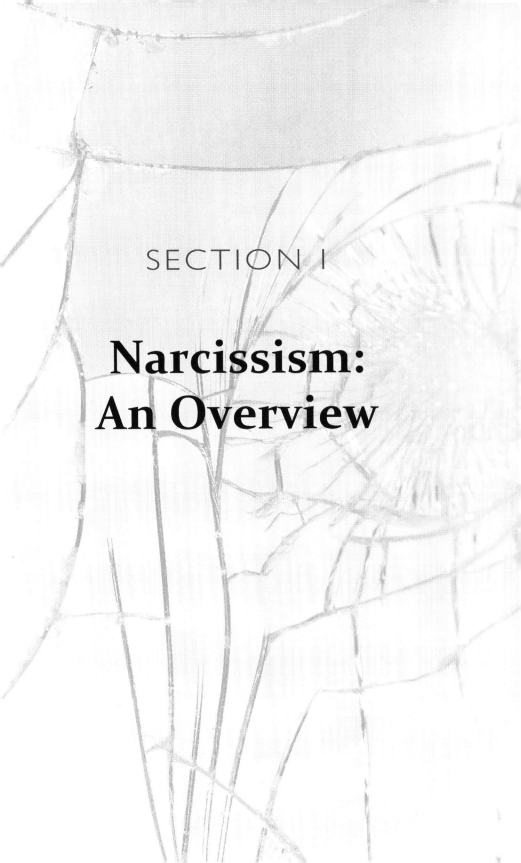

SECTION I

Narcissism: An Overview

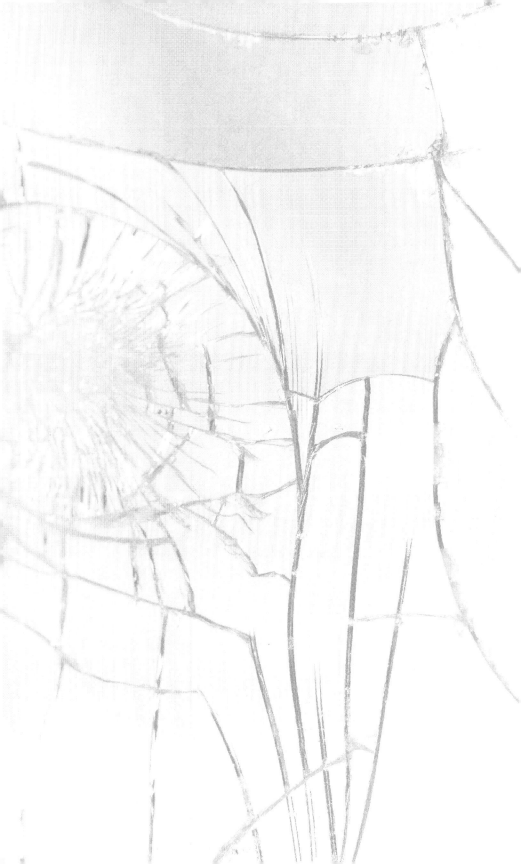

CHAPTER 1

Stuck in the Mirror: A Historical View of the Concept of Narcissism

Origin of the Term

The word *narcissist* historically originates from the Greek legend of Narcissus who looked endlessly into a pond, fell in love with his own image, and pined for it until he died. Narcissus was a hunter in Greek mythology, son of the river god Cephissus and the nymph Liriope. He was a very beautiful young man, and many fell in love with him. However, he showed them only disdain and contempt. One day, while he was hunting in the woods, the nymph Echo spotted him and immediately fell for him. When Narcissus sensed that someone was following him, Echo eventually revealed herself and tried to hug him. He pushed her away and told her not to disturb him. Echo, in despair, roamed around the woods for the rest of her life. She wilted away until all that remained of her was the sound of her echo.

Nemesis, the goddess of retribution and revenge, learned what had happened and decided to punish Narcissus for his behavior. She led him to a pool, where he saw his reflection in the water and fell in love with it. At first, he didn't realize that it was just his reflection, but when he understood, he plunged into despair that the love that he longed for would never materialize. Eventually he withered away and died, leaving behind the comely white flower that is still known as the narcissus.

From this perspective, you can define narcissism as self-love or preoccupation with yourself. Narcissus was not capable of loving anyone else because of the excessive and exclusive love that he felt for himself. This myth was a precursor to the idea that narcissists really can't love because of their inability to feel or relate to anyone's emotions other than their own. His rejection of Echo was a manifestation of his inability to allow anyone into his heart, because his only focus was on himself to the exclusion of all others.

Related Concepts

Hubris

Philosophers throughout history have explored the idea of excessive self-admiration. In Ancient Greece, the idea was known as "hubris," a state of extreme arrogance and overwhelming pride that pushes people so far that they lose touch with reality. Hubris often indicates a loss of contact with what is actually true about yourself, and an overestimation of your own competence, accomplishments, or capabilities. Contrary to common wisdom, hubris is not necessarily associated with high self-esteem, but instead it relates to highly fluctuating or insufficient self-esteem—the gap between inflated self-perception and a more modest reality.

Self-Love

Through the years, other related concepts have emerged that warrant inspection. Early writers saw "self-love" as a pernicious element of personality that can be toxic to your life and relationships. Shakespeare wrote in a 1609 sonnet, "self-love...feed'st thy light's flame with self-substantial fuel." He further stated, "The sin of self-love posseseth all mine eye, and all my soul, and all my every part. And for this sin there is no remedy. It is grounded inward in my heart." He is clearly referring to the fact that self-love is all consuming, and it leaves little room in the heart for anything else.

Sir Frances Bacon, the 16th century English philosopher who was the father of the scientific method, explained, "It is the nature of extreme self-lovers, as they will set a house on fire, and it were but to roast their eggs…" Clearly, these early writers were attuned to the concept of narcissism as destructive self-love.

Egotism

Egotism is yet another term closely related to narcissism, generally regarded as the drive to maintain and enhance favorable views of yourself. It features an inflated opinion of one's personal features and importance. Egotists place themselves at the center of the world, with no concern for others and an overwhelming focus on the "me."

This includes those people the egotist supposedly loves and feels close to, except that the egotist subjectively sets the terms that govern the relationship. In his classic *Leaves of Grass*, Walt Whitman wrote, "I know perfectly well my own egotism, and know my omnivorous word, and would fetch you whoever you are, flush with myself." Egotists are so self-focused that they consume anyone in their personal sphere to meet their needs for attention and power.

Conceit

The Merriam-Webster dictionary defines conceited people as those who have or show an overly high opinion of themselves. They may have an "excessively favorable opinion of their own ability, importance, wit, status, or standing." (dictionary.com) If you're always boasting about yourself, or you can't stop talking about your achievements, possessions, or virtues, you are probably conceited. Your friends may also complain about your arrogance, vanity, or egotism, that is, if they stick around. (vocabulary.com)

Conceit obviously relates to the concept of narcissism, since one of its core elements is a distorted, inflated self-image, often used as a defense mechanism to cover underlying feelings of inadequacy and defectiveness. Conceited people see themselves as superior. They look down on other people to soothe their own underlying sense of inadequacy.

Arrogance

Arrogance, according to Merriam-Webster, means "to exaggerate or to be disposed to exaggerate one's worth or importance, often in an overbearing manner," or "to show an attitude of superiority." Dictionary.com defines arrogance as "making claims or pretentions to superior importance or rights," and being "overbearingly assuming; insolently proud."

Arrogant people make it quite obvious that they have superior intelligence, attractiveness, and success in comparison to anyone else's. They make no secret of their feelings about themselves or others, and they're perfectly comfortable expressing their judgmental, self-inflated attitudes to other people around them.

Megalomania

As opposed to the previous concepts related to narcissism, megalomania is more of a psychiatric disorder, or mental illness, in that it involves a clear stepping out of reality. It often manifests with delusions of grandeur or omnipotence and a sense of unlimited power and brilliance. People with this disorder often see themselves as being some special person, perhaps as G-d, the president, or a famous celebrity. Mental health professionals generally see megalomania as a psychotic illness, rather than a personality disorder, although the traits usually associated with it are often seen in connection with narcissism, e.g., an inflated sense of self, an unreasonable need for power, and an excessive focus on oneself.

Megalomania is most often found within the context of mental illnesses such as schizophrenia, bipolar disorder, delusional disorder, or paranoid disorder. It can also have a clear biological cause and, in some cases, may indicate a brain tumor or a serious biochemical imbalance.

Theorists see all of these personality and psychological constructs as pathological parallels to narcissism. This implies that if you focus on or love yourself to the extent that it limits your ability to focus on or love others, by definition, you're being narcissistic. To put it another way, if you focus exclusively on loving and admiring yourself, that feeling supplants the love that a mature, other-centered individual would naturally feel for another person who is important and dear.

Development of Narcissism as a Psychological Disorder

Historically, earlier psychoanalysts developed an interest in narcissistic behavior at the beginning of the 20th century. In 1911, psychoanalyst Otto Rank was the first to identify narcissism as a psychological concept, describing it as associated with self-admiration and vanity. In 1914, Sigmund Freud published a paper entitled "On Narcissism: An Introduction," wherein he introduced the idea that narcissism is actually a natural method the brain uses to create self-defense barriers. In that paper, Freud did not conceptualize narcissism as a form of pathology, but rather as a benign defense mechanism that preserves the stability of the ego.

He suggested that exclusive self-love might not be as abnormal as previously thought, and it might even be a common component in the human psyche. He argued that narcissism "is the libidinal complement to the egoism of the instinct of self-preservation" or, more simply, the desire and energy that drives a person's instinct to survive. He referred to this as primary narcissism.

Later, Freud conceptualized secondary narcissism as a pathological entity that causes self-focus beyond the early years of personality development. This involves the libido turning onto oneself, making a person his or her own object of sexual pleasure. The exclusive focus on self in adulthood, as opposed to paying attention to relationships with other people, is the key concept here that differentiates normal, if not healthy, self-love from pathological self-preoccupation.

Other earlier psychoanalysts dealt with narcissism based on "object relations theory." Psychoanalyst Melanie Klein, who initiated the concept of object relations, proposed that the quality of our early relations with the primary objects in our lives, usually our mothers, influences our personality development. According to Klein, the bonding people experience in their early years affects how they bond with others later in life. Klein found that narcissistic internal structures and relationships arise in an effort to escape fear and insecurity through using other people to confirm a sense of grandiosity.

In other words, according to Klein, people with impaired early object relations become anxious and insecure, and then they degrade others as a way to artificially inflate their own egos and to fulfill the need to feel superior.

In 1967, narcissism was finally recognized as a formal disorder by psychoanalyst Otto Kernberg, who expanded it into three branches: Normal Adult Narcissism, which is akin to Freud's primary narcissism; Normal Infantile Narcissism, which represents the normative self-centeredness associated with early childhood; and Pathological Narcissism, which forms the basis of the diagnosis of narcissism as a personality disorder.

In 1968, psychoanalyst Heinz Kohut introduced the term "Narcissistic Personality Disorder" or NPD. He looked further into Freud and Kernberg's previous ideas, and elaborated more deeply on the concept of a narcissistic individual, a condition he was the first to describe as being a "narcissist."

By the 1980s, the third edition of *The Diagnostic and Statistical Manual of Mental Disorders* officially included Narcissistic Personality Disorder, delineating specific standards for the diagnosis of NPD. It established nine criteria, with the understanding that a patient had to meet at least five to be formally diagnosed. This book will describe these criteria more fully in the next chapter.

More contemporary thinking views the concept of narcissism as having a number of connotations, depending on context. The most common form of the word is colloquially used to describe a self-centered or self-absorbed person. When someone uses the word "narcissist," it frequently describes a person who sees life as being "all about him/her." People commonly characterize narcissists as those who enjoy talking about themselves, have little interest in what others say, and are preoccupied with their own status, attention, and admiration.

Clinically speaking, however, the concept of narcissism has developed into a much broader focus than self-centeredness, although that is arguably at the core of the disorder. The term generally refers to a disruption of personality development, in which the person fails to make the transition from the normative self-centeredness of childhood and adolescence to an age-appropriate ability to focus on the needs and feelings of others, along with the need to be in a mutually loving relationship. In this sense, we view narcissism as a sort of "arrested development," in which individuals get stuck in earlier stages of development, so they fail to enter adulthood at an emotional and relational level.

Now that we've looked at how the concept of narcissism has developed over time, let's consider what we're really talking about when we refer to narcissism, so you can see and understand how it might apply to you.

CHAPTER 2

How Do I Know if I Am One?
Diagnostic Considerations

Diagnostic Criteria

When clinicians (mental health professionals such as psychiatrists, psychologists, licensed clinical social workers, or counselors) try to identify a particular psychological disorder, they use a reference book called the *Diagnostic and Statistical Manual of Mental Disorders* (commonly referred to as the *DSM*). This manual describes various diagnostic criteria that are essential in arriving at a clinical diagnosis of mental disorders, including Narcissistic Personality Disorder (NPD). More importantly, it describes in detail how the disorder usually manifests in people, as well as its frequency in the population and common coexisting disorders. This chapter will describe the criteria that professionals use so that you can try to identify if any of the descriptors apply to you and your personality. This book will also help you differentiate between having some traits of the disorder or having a full-blown case. It will also discuss the incidence rate in the general population.

One of the challenges you will face in determining if any of these descriptors apply to you is mustering the ability to see yourself objectively, with intellectual honesty, and not relying on your own perceptions, which can often be distorted and inaccurate. People who are described as being narcissistic in various ways often don't see themselves as others do. So, if you're able to be objective about yourself, and some narcissists definitely can do that, read the criteria below and see if you can identify which ones apply to you. If you are not sure if you're capable of being completely objective, ask your significant other which of the criteria s/he has experienced in your relationship.

The *DSM-V's* (the DSM fifth edition) definition and diagnostic criteria, as written in the most current version of the manual, are:

GENERAL DEFINITION
OF NARCISSISTIC PERSONALITY DISORDER

"A pervasive pattern of grandiosity (in fantasy or behavior), need for admiration, and lack of empathy, beginning by early adulthood and present in a variety of contexts, as indicated by five (or more) of the following:

Diagnostic Criteria

1. Has a grandiose sense of self-importance (e.g., exaggerates achievements and talents, expects to be recognized as superior without commensurate achievements).

2. Is preoccupied with fantasies of unlimited success, power, brilliance, beauty, or ideal love.

3. Believes that he or she is "special" and unique and can only be understood by, or should only associate with, other special or high-status people (or institutions).

4. Requires excessive admiration.

5. Has a sense of entitlement, i.e., unreasonable expectations of especially favorable treatment or automatic compliance with his or her expectations.

6. Is interpersonally exploitative, i.e., takes advantage of others to achieve his or her own ends.

7. Lacks empathy: is unwilling to recognize or identify with the feelings and needs of others.

8. Is often envious of others or believes that others are envious of him or her.

9. Shows arrogant, haughty behaviors or attitudes.

Disorder Versus Traits

According to the *DSM*, a clinical diagnosis requires having at least five of the above criteria. So, if you're able to identify at least five of them as something you or your significant other can relate to, then you would qualify for a diagnosis of Narcissistic Personality Disorder. I know, it's not exactly like winning the lottery, but if you've been struggling with relationships for a good part of your life, it's difficult, if not impossible, to change that reality if you can't identify the problem. These criteria can help you understand what has kept you from being successful in your relationships. While this realization may be uncomfortable for you, I hope you can also understand that it's a necessary prerequisite for real change. This exercise will also help you identify the unique ways that narcissism manifests itself in you, since each person is an individual, and it's rare for two people to be narcissistic in exactly the same ways. It is also important to know that there are other characteristics of narcissistic personalities that are not included in these diagnostic criteria, such as hypersensitivity to criticism and distortions of reality to fit one's narrative of defensiveness. You can use these personality criteria to help you understand your narcissistic profile and track your progress as the therapeutic process unfolds.

Many of you reading this book will see that you manifest one or two of these criteria, but you may not identify with the rest of the descriptions listed. If, after checking that out with others, you find that this is true, then, in all probability, you don't have the full-blown disorder, but, instead, you may have *narcissistic traits*. This means that you are probably not a narcissist, per se, but rather someone who, under certain defined circumstances, can *become* narcissistic. For example, you may be able to be other-centered, empathetic, and successful in non-intimate relationships, such as with friends, colleagues, or clients. However, with your significant other, who may trigger old wounds from your past, you become defensive and judgmental, and you can't understand his or her perspective or feelings once you are in that state. That would be a good example of having narcissistic traits that manifest in certain situations, but not in others.

The distinction between having a personality disorder and having some of its traits is crucial in terms of your self-awareness, as well as your ability to change and accomplish your therapeutic goals. Generally speaking, it's far easier to transition out of narcissism at the trait level, as opposed to the disorder level. In someone who just has traits, narcissism is not interwoven into the fabric of the personality and not imbedded as pervasive patterns of thinking, emotions, and behavior. Therefore, the challenge of change is not as difficult as it is with someone who has many characteristics of the disorder and has been formally diagnosed. Even if you are diagnosed with NPD, that doesn't mean you can't change, or at least modify, your personality. It just means that you'll probably need to work much harder and longer to accomplish the goal of being effective and successful in your relationships. Conversely, if you have only a few traits, you'll probably be more able to modify them more quickly and less painfully, although achieving the goal of being free of narcissism in your personality will still involve a lot of work on your part.

Incidence and Prevalence in American Culture

According to the *DSM-V*, Narcissistic Personality Disorder occurs in approximately 2% to 16% of the population in clinical settings, and between 0.5% and 1% of the general population. More than half of those diagnosed are men. However, in 2008, a national epidemiological survey of almost 35,000 adults found that the prevalence rate of NPD in the general population was actually much higher: 6.2%, with men having rates of 7.7%, and women 4.8%. If you consider that, according to the United States' census, the nation's population is 325.7 million, this figure translates to approximately 20 million narcissists running around, wreaking havoc in our society. This is significant in that narcissism obviously isn't uncommon, so if you relate to this chapter, you aren't alone.

When the revised version of the *DSM-V* was published in 2013, the prevalence rate was still 6.2% in community samples, which shows that this relatively high rate is apparently constant.

The question is: Why is this disorder so prevalent? Many experts have written about today's narcissistic society, which has values of materialism and entitlement that are closely associated with narcissism. The media pushes countless advertisements for luxury items encouraging those who fall prey to its manipulations to "go ahead and indulge, you deserve it." Whether it's luxury cars, expensive watches, designer clothes, or exotic vacations, the media encourages Americans—and we often convince ourselves—to believe that we're entitled to splurge, even if we can't really afford it.

Some argue that the political system encourages citizens to expect "entitlement" payments from the government. Some of these entitlements, such as Social Security, aren't really entitlements in the true narcissistic sense of the word, because those who benefit from Social Security actually paid into the system throughout their working lives. Now they receive benefits that they earned and deserve. However, opponents of public assistance may argue that some people unduly feel entitled to government benefits. Does the American system lead people to feel too entitled? The degree to which this sense of entitlement has permeated society remains to be seen. Does it go to the extent that it contributes to the prevalence of NPD? No one knows for sure.

Finally, as we will discuss in the next chapter, narcissistic parents often raise narcissistic children, so it's a self-perpetuating phenomenon. Since our society apparently includes so many narcissistic people, the number of people affected by this disorder can logically only continue to rise exponentially. It's no wonder, then, that the rate of narcissism is so high, relatively speaking, in the United States.

CHAPTER 3

How Did I Get This Way?
The Causes of Narcissism

In general, when someone asks me if people become who they are because of genetic factors, modeling by parents, traumatic events, or cultural influences, I usually just say "yes." In almost all cases, some sort of interactive effect involving some or all of these factors influences personality development. However, depending on which experts you read and their theoretical orientation, you will see varying opinions on the relative importance of each factor in influencing the development of personality and—of particular relevance to this book—the development of personality disorders.

Historical Overview of Personality Theory

From what I have studied about the etiology (causes) of personality pathology over the years that I've been involved in psychology, the focus of the literature on this subject has evolved in the last number of decades. When I first learned about psychology in the early 1970s, most of the discussion about personality emanated from classic Freudian theory or, at least, from neo-Freudian theorists such as Jung and Adler. They posited (simply put) that personality development resulted from intrapsychic or unconscious processes stemming from the complexities in our relationships with our parents. Without getting into academic detail, this line of thinking—which involves such concepts as the id, ego, superego, collective unconscious, and psychoanalytic therapy—dominated the field of psychology for most of the 20th century until the behavioral theorists became more popular in the 1960s and 1970s.

The behavioral theorists focused on learned or conditioned behaviors as the critical elements in personality development. Behaviorists paid attention to identifying behavioral antecedents and changing behavior, using behavior modification therapies as a means of personality change. The 1980s and 1990s saw the emergence of social learning theory as a new focus of personality development. During this time, researchers also identified early trauma as an important contribution to psychopathology, especially within the context of personality disorders. However, the factor that has emerged most strongly over the last number of decades is a new appreciation of the role of genetics in how we become who we are.

Genetics

Understanding the role of genes in what color our eyes are, the texture and color of our hair, our height, and other obvious physical features is far easier than understanding the much more complex role that genetics plays in how our personalities develop. However, research on genetics and personality has become more and more convincing in terms of how we inherit certain personality characteristics, regardless of our early experiences. Much of the research that substantiates that genetics is far more significant than expected in determining how personalities develop comes from studies of identical (monozygotic) twins. Researchers study twins who were separated at birth and raised in vastly different cultures, with different family dynamics, socioeconomic status, and parenting environments, but yet end up with extraordinarily similar personality traits. A landmark study done in Minnesota between 1979 and 1999 looked at identical twins who were separated at birth. Years later, the twins showed a remarkable amount of congruence in such personality factors as temperament, religiosity, and introversion or extroversion, even though they were not brought up together. Clearly, genetics plays a significant role in such cases.

In addition, personality types seem to run in families. How often have you seen a person whose personality reminds you of his or her aunt or grandfather? It's not uncommon for a child with basically normal parents who were not particularly narcissistic to develop strong narcissistic personality traits. If you look closely back a generation, often people saw one or more of that narcissistic person's grandparents as being "difficult" or "strong-willed," probably catchphrases for narcissism.

Sometimes, children who are raised by the same parents in roughly the same environmental circumstances develop completely different personalities. Often, one or more children stand out in a family as being challenging to raise because of their narcissistic traits, such as self-centeredness or selfishness, whereas the other children are more normative, if not the opposite from their difficult sibling. Many parents with this family dynamic describe these children as having been constitutionally difficult or "tough to handle" from the earliest of ages. They could tell that these kids were different. To explain this phenomenon, they often identify a trait that they can trace as running in one or both families. In fact, the tide in research into the determinants of personality is strongly leaning toward hereditary factors as being more influential than a person's early environment.

CASE EXAMPLE 1: JULIA

Julia* was the oldest daughter of elderly parents, Janet and Leonard, who came for therapy to get a better understanding of her and to seek support in dealing with her. From as early as they can remember, Julia was a difficult, self-absorbed, excessively willful child. She had to have her way, or she would have a temper tantrum or endlessly sulk in her bedroom. She was emotionally abusive to her two younger sisters, whom she resented because her parents paid attention to them as babies or toddlers. That took attention—and, in her mind, love—away from her. As she grew older, she became an oppositional teenager and made life a living hell for her parents. Rules did not matter to Julia. Her relationships with her schoolmates and neighbors were always problematic, and she had a strong pattern of alienating everyone in her orbit.

I met Julia when she was in her late 40s, having been divorced twice. She was alienated from her teenage daughter, whom she allowed (encouraged) to live with her father, because she "couldn't deal with her." Julia's mother reported that she showed little, if any, interest in her daughter's welfare, and felt no maternal instincts, responsibility, or affection for her, preferring to focus on building her career in music instead. She was emotionally abusive to her parents, incapable of demonstrating any empathy toward them though her mother was infirm and wheelchair-bound due to a degenerative neurological disorder. When I met with Julia, she portrayed herself as the misunderstood victim of her insufferable parents who refused to let her be an adult. She felt entitled to interminable financial support, and resisted getting a job, because it would interfere with her career and her ability to develop her unusual musical talent—yet, she was angry at her parents for still making her feel like a dependent child. Julia was a textbook narcissist.

What was unusual about this situation was that Janet and Leonard, by any measure, were excellent parents. They were educated, loving, and attentive parents who knew how and when to draw limits with their other children, who developed into successful, loving adults. Leonard, a kind, considerate Midwesterner, and Janet, a special education teacher from California who had the patience of a saint, were bewildered about how they could have produced a child with such a disturbed personality since they utilized the same parenting approach that produced their other highly well-adjusted children.

The missing link to this puzzle emerged only after quite a number of sessions when I thought to ask Janet and Leonard about their parents. Leonard's mother was an angry, self-centered, hypercritical woman who was not emotionally available to her eight children or to her husband. Instead, she fancifully pursued her dream of being a famous singer. She spent an inordinate amount of time on singing lessons the family could not afford, practicing, trying out for gigs, and going out with friends to concerts, singing festivals, and the like. When she was home, she actually made things worse, ranting and raving about whatever inane misstep one of the children or her husband inadvertently committed. She invariably launched vitriolic attacks on her latest victim. Janet reported that in her later years her mother-in-law was so malevolent that they had to cut off all contact. She was so abusive to them both that she caused an inordinate amount of stress and discord within their otherwise good marriage.

What became obvious at that point was that Julia presented a clear case of a genetic link that strongly suggested that her toxic personality traits were not caused by parenting or environmental factors, but were more likely due, unfortunately, to inheriting strong narcissistic personality traits from her paternal grandmother. As a result, she developed a full-blown Narcissistic Personality Disorder, despite her parents' best efforts to raise her in a home filled with love, amid reasonable expectations of responsibility and respect. Her grandmother died shortly before Julia was born, and she never had the chance to meet her, thus negating the theory that her grandmother's modeling of narcissistic behaviors may have influenced Julia's personality development. It was a matter of nature vs. nurture, and in this case, nature won.

So, what does this all mean to you? Well, it may be a bit sobering to realize that you were "born this way," a daunting thought in terms of change. First of all, personality traits are rarely as one-dimensional as Julia's. Heredity is often just a part of the puzzle in terms of explaining how you became you. We will deal with that shortly. But it's important to know that the psychotherapeutic techniques we'll discuss in Chapter 15 are effective in modifying unhealthy personality traits and disorders, even if they are genetic in origin.

The bottom line is that if you want to be more successful in your life, understanding that you may have inherited unhealthy traits can help you understand their origins. It may also give you a strong impetus to "not be like Grandma Sara," who made the entire family miserable with her demanding, critical personality, and inordinate need for attention. Just this recognition alone can increase the motivation for, and the chances of, real change.

Family Dynamics

You don't have to be a Freudian psychoanalyst to understand that, despite the predominating influence of genetics, parenting and family dynamics can affect personality development in general, and the development of narcissism in particular. Generally speaking, narcissism can develop from either extreme along the continuum of attention and nurturing. Many, if not most, of my patients had parents who were neglectful, self-focused, or abusive on the one hand or, on the other hand, overly indulgent and unable to set limits. They made their children feel like the center of the universe. Those who experienced neglectful or abusive parenting learn early on that "no one was home" emotionally, so if they wanted to get their needs met, they had to focus on themselves.

Such parents failed to build their children up emotionally, so the kids developed narcissism to defend against their deep-seated feelings of inadequacy and inferiority (more on that later in Chapter 7). Instead of being aware of and connected to these feelings, individuals who deploy the narcissistic defense mechanism can detach from negative feelings about themselves, and artificially "pump themselves up" through self-aggrandizement, grandiosity, and self-victimization. Thus they deflect blame for their failings onto others. As we'll discuss also in Chapter 7, other defense mechanisms kick in as well. Neglectful or abusive parents damage their children in a way that brings out the narcissism in their personalities by forcing them to cope with otherwise overwhelming feelings of self-hate and underlying worthlessness.

A word about parental neglect is in order here to clarify this concept. An important conceptual difference separates benevolent or benign neglect from malevolent, or malicious neglect. Parents who basically mean well and don't intend to neglect their children may practice benign neglect. Such parents often are extremely limited in their ability to parent because they are overwhelmed, emotionally disturbed, or limited in other ways, and just have nothing to give. Such neglect does not necessarily produce narcissism in their offspring, but it can, given the right circumstances and genetic loading. However, malevolent neglect, a more purposeful or intentional desire to withhold love or to willfully punish or wound a child because of a perceived slight or disrespect, is more likely to damage a developing child's personality. It often creates the type of narcissism that serves to protect the child from feeling the pain and insecurity arising from such parenting.

It's also not unusual to find a situation in which a parent (or parents) are so fragile and self-absorbed—and thus unable to do much in the way of parenting—that a child (or children) take on the role of being a parent, not only with their siblings, but with their parents themselves. This is the "parentified child." Children of narcissistic parents often overly focus on making sure they don't trigger their quick-to-anger parent(s) and on trying to meet their needs.

This usually leads to one of two outcomes in the child's personality development later in life. Parentified children often become narcissistic, blaming their parents for their problems and shortcomings, while mired in anger and self-absorption. This is often the result of a common combination of genetic loading, parental modeling of narcissistic behaviors, and the development of narcissism as a defense mechanism to mask underlying feelings of inferiority and self-hatred caused by their narcissistic parents' criticism and rejection.

Alternatively, these children become "anti-narcissistic," or pathologically other-centered, with little ability to focus on their own feeling or needs, and constantly worried about upsetting other people. Anti-narcissistic individuals usually have no core, or sense of self, and are extremely external in their locus of control, their general orientation about what they allow to affect them. Anti-narcissists become conditioned early in their development to focus on their parents, or on other fragile and labile family members, in order to escape their wrath and to protect the family's equilibrium. Other family members often see them as altruistic, and they may be so, but my experience has led me to see these individuals beyond the surface. Usually, some latent or compartmentalized narcissistic traits eventually unfold, often under some environmental context that elicits a narcissistic reaction.

CASE EXAMPLE 2: CYNTHIA AND LYLE

Cynthia was an attractive woman in her early 50s who came in for treatment to deal with a depressive episode that resulted from her husband of 25 years leaving her for a younger woman. His betrayal shocked her, since she had been a loyal wife, and they had been successful business partners, and had together built what she had thought was a collaborative, successful life. In truth, her husband, Lyle, was a profoundly arrogant, controlling man. He came from a wealthy, powerful family who projected their sense of superiority on other people when they interacted. Lyle had an unduly strong influence on most of their decisions, from which friends they would socialize with, at which restaurants they would dine, and even which clothes she would wear. Cynthia seemed drawn to Lyle because this dynamic was familiar to her. Her family was a deeply judgmental, critical group of people, who conditioned her to believe that she was defective and inadequate throughout her life. Her parents blatantly favored her brothers over her, and they, in turn, made her feel inferior and rather stupid, although she excelled throughout her academic career, eventually becoming a successful rheumatologist.

Cynthia was actually a lovely, charming, intensely altruistic, and ethical person. She was sensitive and generous to her friends, almost to an extreme, and would always put others' needs before her own. She was quite preoccupied with what other people felt about her, and she worked hard to cultivate friendships based on what she gave to or did for her friends. In her marriage, she was overly deferential to Lyle, and enabled him to be in charge of their finances, relationships, and business decisions, although she had more people skills and medical expertise than he had.

In this case history, Lyle developed a Narcissistic Personality Disorder due to a combination of highly indulgent, permissive parenting, and the sense throughout his developmental years that he was the center of the universe because of his family's social and financial position. Cynthia, on the other hand, developed an anti-narcissistic personality, due to early conditioning that forced her to be constantly in a state of vigilance to ensure that she would not incur the wrath or degradation of her family. Yet, at times, Cynthia's underlying narcissistic traits would emerge, given specific circumstances when she, too, would be highly critical of others who failed to live up to her often unrealistically high expectations. She could also be highly sensitive to criticism and very defensive in reacting to comments she saw as critical, even though those who were making the comments did not intend to be critical or to make her uncomfortable. Cynthia was a prototypical anti-narcissistic/narcissistic combination, whose lack of a real core and a sense of self resulted in her being devastated after her husband left her.

Trauma

Children generally need a safe, secure childhood to develop into healthy, caring, nurturing adults. When children feel that their emotional needs are met, that "their buckets are full," they have room to explore their ability to fill the buckets of other people in their lives. When we feel secure within ourselves, we can step outside of ourselves to be vulnerable and to focus on the needs of others.

However, when children experience physical, emotional, or sexual trauma, their personality development can derail. This can become the formative element behind the development of a personality disorder, especially when the trauma is ongoing and results from family experiences. An abusive, dysfunctional family life, in which instability and chaos are the norm, interferes with healthy personality development and can be a causal factor in personality issues later in life. Trauma can often lead to the development of Borderline Personality Disorder (BPD), a serious condition characterized by mood instability, emotional dysregulation, identity disturbance, and transient psychosis. In my years in practice, I've never treated someone with BPD who hadn't experienced some sort of severe acute or, more often, chronic trauma in childhood. What is significant for our discussion, however, is that narcissism is almost always a significant component of BPD, and is invariably a component of the individual's personality structure at some level. Every patient with BPD has at least some narcissistic personality features, but the reverse is not the case. Just because you are struggling with narcissism doesn't mean that you're necessarily dealing with BPD, as well. Trauma can, and usually does, have a significant bearing on the development of a personality disorder. Narcissism is a case in point.

In addition to abuse and neglect in the context of family dynamics, trauma involving your peers can also deeply affect your self-esteem and sense of self in ways that can lead to the development of narcissism. Quite a few patients with whom I've worked over the years could trace the damage to their personality back to sustained, ongoing bullying during their formative, most sensitive years of adolescence and pre-adolescence. The shame and humiliation that results from bullying can cause lasting effects on your self-confidence and self-image, often resulting in the development of narcissistic defenses to protect against deep, painful emotions. This period often comes during the most vulnerable years in a developing child's life. When a child is a victim of bullying, whether at school, outside of school hours, or on social media, the effects can be long-lasting, and deeply damaging.

Relational Trauma

"Relational trauma" refers to the trauma that comes from upsetting or shocking behavior in interpersonal relationships. Young children find trauma especially disturbing when it originates from people who are supposed to be safe for them to be around and supportive of them, such as their parents, teachers, or friends. Young children are particularly vulnerable in terms of their developing brains. Imprinting traumatic experiences can cause long-lasting effects in terms of personality, psychological functioning, relationships, and spirituality.

CASE EXAMPLE 3: AARON

Aaron, a handsome, dynamic man in his mid-30s, came for therapy to deal with the breakup of his latest marriage, his third after two explosive divorces. His business partner, a former patient of mine, encouraged Aaron to come in for help, since he was going down the same path as in his previous divorces. His partner wanted to prevent some of the same fiascos that had occurred previously.

Initially, Aaron presented as an angry, bitter man, who felt victimized, again, by another difficult, manipulative woman who was trying to take financial advantage of him. His sole focus was on how his wife was reacting irrationally to his infrequent fits of rage, in which he was verbally and physically abusive toward her, even to the point of causing her bodily harm. He was able to see only what she did to trigger him, and how out of control she became as a result of his reactions. He was incapable of introspection and looking at what he was doing to create the dynamic that caused her reactions. In Aaron's view, the couple's problem was her emotional reactions, and how frustrating she was to him, not his attitude or behavior.

In discussing his history, it was apparent that he, himself, was a victim of abuse and neglect, at home, and in school. He grew up in a small town in eastern Canada, the only son of Holocaust survivors who ended up there after World War II, as a result of the Canadian government's efforts to disperse refugees across the country, rather than having them settle only in centralized communities in big cities. As a result, he was in one of only a few survivor families in the town, which also had a small Jewish community in general.

Aaron's father was a shell of a man. He had survived several concentration camps, and he lost his entire family to the ravages of the war. He barely spoke to Aaron, and was not involved much in raising him or in his life, in general. His mother, in contrast, was an overbearing, emotionally explosive woman. She was also a severely traumatized Holocaust survivor who suffered unspeakable humiliation and trauma at the hands of the Nazis in her native Poland. She was forcibly taken from her parents as a young girl, and she watched her father being killed before her eyes. Later, a guard raped her at a concentration camp and left her to die. She escaped to the surrounding forest, where she managed to survive more than a year and a half before being liberated.

Aaron's formative memories focused mostly on explosive episodes at home. When something triggered his mother, she would rage about one thing or another. When I asked him to relate his most painful memory, he told the story about when he was riding his bike home from school on an icy winter day, and he skidded into an oncoming car, which hit him straight on, throwing him off the bicycle, and damaging it severely. His side was severely bruised, and he fractured a bone in his leg, as a result of being thrown to the ground so violently. The car sped away, and no other cars were around to stop and help him. He picked himself up, and hobbled his way home. When he rang the doorbell, his mother saw the smashed bicycle, and flew into an uncontrolled rage. She slapped him across the top of his head, and yelled at him for destroying his bicycle because it had cost them so much money to buy. She never asked him what happened, or asked him about his injuries, but just stormed off to the kitchen, leaving Aaron with his father sitting lamely on a chair in the living room, paralyzed by inaction.

In addition, non-Jewish students bullied Aaron at school, joking about his strange-sounding Polish last name (which he has since changed to a shorter, Anglicized version). His Jewish classmates taunted him even more mercilessly about his primitive-looking parents and shoddy clothing. He was mocked, ridiculed, and often beaten up, for no reason at all, other than because he was such an easy target. Because he was short, he found it difficult to defend himself, and he often cried himself home, knowing that he wouldn't get much comfort there, either.

Not surprisingly, Aaron had a lot of suppressed rage. As part of his effort to submerge the deep feelings of shame and defectiveness from his childhood, he developed a severe Narcissistic Personality Disorder. He became obsessed with being financially successful, and eventually built a large luxury auto dealership. At work, he was harshly critical, reactive, and extremely angry and defensive. He could never acknowledge being at fault or bearing any responsibility in his work-related relationships. A clear pattern emerged in his personal life. Women would be attracted to his rugged good looks and success, as well as his wit and charm, but after marriage, his darker narcissistic traits would quickly emerge, causing the couple to descend into a spiral of criticism, blame, frustration, and finally alienation.

This pattern recurred over and over again, but this time, Aaron was finally willing to take a painful look inside himself, and to try to understand the dynamics of his childhood trauma, his personality, and the relationships that ultimately failed as a result. After intense Eye Movement Desensitization and Reprocessing (EMDR) treatment for trauma, as well as deep insight-oriented therapy, and relationship skills training, Aaron was able to embark on a healthy journey toward a successful relationship. [See Case Example 33 for more details of Aaron's EMDR treatment.]

CHAPTER 4

How Bad Is It?
Ways of Describing the Nature and Impact of Narcissism

Severity

As is the case in all personality disorders, there is a continuum of severity that describes the intensity of narcissism's impact on a person's interpersonal functioning. This continuum also describes the impact of the disorder on the people with whom the narcissist interacts. Generally, you can describe personality disorders along the lines of mild, moderate, and severe, with allowances for sub-categories such as mild to moderate, moderate to severe, and very severe.

Mild

Individuals for whom the trauma, neglect, or overindulgence that contributed to damaging their personalities wasn't too intense often reflect a mild form of narcissism that affects their ability to succeed in relationships, but not to a significant degree. They're generally benignly self-focused, in that they have difficulty understanding other people's perspectives or being sensitive to others' feelings, but they're otherwise regarded as "good people." Milder forms of narcissism often are easier to modify in therapy than other forms, since these are often, though not always, highly correlated with the ability to change (see Chapter 5).

CASE EXAMPLE 4: CHRIS

Chris was a 36-year-old, newly married attorney who came from a family of successful attorneys. His family expressed clear expectations early on that he would follow in his father's and siblings' footsteps, and enter the legal profession, even though he did not possess the natural interest in law that his relatives seemed to have. Instead, his passion was sports, and he secretly wanted to develop his passion for hockey, which would never have been acceptable to his highly educated, achievement-oriented family. His parents were driven and ambitious, but overall they also tended to be attentive and supportive. He ultimately acquiesced to the family plan, but struggled throughout law school, and was generally seen as the weak link in the family's criminal law practice in Boston. He was well aware of his relative inadequacies, and tried to compensate by being loud and brash about the things in which he excels, such as knowing sports trivia, playing poker, and driving fast sports cars.

After being a bachelor well into his 30s, Chris finally found a young woman who met his expectations. After a long courtship, they were married in an elaborate church ceremony followed by a reception at his parents' country club. Jen was a tall, beautiful, interior designer who thought that she could tolerate Chris's idiosyncratic interests and behaviors. She quickly found that his self-indulgences and insensitivity to her needs were becoming a problem. When she expressed her feelings about these issues, Chris was bewildered and confused. After much discussion, he agreed to go to therapy to work on their relationship. After several months of psychotherapy, in which the therapist worked with Chris to develop better awareness of Jen's feelings and needs—including making efforts to tone down the extravagances that made her uncomfortable—they both felt that their relationship had improved considerably. Chris was able to make significant changes to the extent that Jen was quite happy with the results of therapy and with Chris as her partner.

Chris is considered to be mildly narcissistic. His case is mild even though some features of his personality were definitely self-oriented and he engaged in attention-seeking behavior. However, he was able to see quickly that he was affecting his wife's well-being, and he was non-defensive in agreeing to work on himself. Left to his own devices, he was clueless as to the detrimental effect he was having on his relationships, but once he became aware, he earnestly worked on modifying his self-centeredness and eliminating the behaviors that were so upsetting to Jen. He also was able to understand readily that his narcissism was an attempt to mask his inadequacies, and he began to work on his self-esteem to eliminate the need to be grandiose in order to artificially pump up his deflated self-concept.

Moderate

People with moderate narcissism can be quite self-focused, critical, defensive, and insensitive to the needs of others, to the extent that their relationships are invariably impaired. However, they have the capacity to work on themselves, usually with the help of a therapist or an effective spouse. They can become aware of the toxicity of their behavior, and their patterns of negative relationships, and can make the transition, to some extent, at least, out of a narcissistic pattern of relating to others and toward healthier, more effective interpersonal interactions.

CASE EXAMPLE 5: BELINDA

Belinda was a twice-divorced, high-end real estate broker. She came in for treatment because her daughter and son-in-law had stopped speaking to her and refused to allow her to have contact with their three daughters. She came into the first session bitterly complaining about how she was being treated, and painting herself as the victim of her selfish daughter Clarissa's sole focus on her own needs and what was good for her family. She was also upset about her "loser" son-in-law Jack's lack of gratitude for all of the financial support she had provided over the years. She further resented that they "couldn't care less" that she was, once again, alone and struggling to find a relationship that worked for her.

When her daughter and son-in-law came in to discuss the breakdown in the relationship, they presented an entirely different picture. They said they decided to end contact only when Belinda's controlling, abusive behavior began to spill onto their daughters, and she started to pull them into her conflict with their parents. Their oldest daughter, Samantha, had revealed to them that Grandma had invited her to come out to lunch on a school day, with a shopping spree afterward to buy clothes that were more stylish than the "rags" that her mother bought her. Belinda would have had to pick Samantha up early from school, so she told Samantha not to tell her "overly controlling" parents about their plans, and to say only that she had to stay late in school.

This was the last straw for Jack and Clarissa, since Belinda had engaged in an endless pattern of intrusiveness and criticism of their parenting, as well as unreasonable demands to put her needs first above those of their family. Belinda typically expected Clarissa to change family plans at the last minute when she invited her or the girls out for lunch or to a social function. Whenever Clarissa declined, Belinda would fly into a rage, expressing contempt for her daughter's lack of respect and sensitivity to her needs as a mother and grandmother. She would also throw into their faces the financial assistance that she had provided over the years as a result of Jack's business setbacks in his struggling family restaurant.

At her second session, after I explained her family's perspective on their conflict, Belinda was, at first, defensive and angry that I would even think of believing their side. After all, they obviously had to justify their horrible treatment of her by telling such distorted lies about her. I reminded her that she had presented for treatment, not her family, and that to succeed in reconciling with them, she would have to acknowledge their perspective and feelings before they could even consider allowing any further contact. Only then did she begin to admit that she sometimes got "too emotional," and then didn't see their side of a disagreement.

After a few sessions, during which she became aware of the damaging effects of her own mother's multiple marriages, unsuitable husbands, and constant uprooting to move to her new stepfathers' locations, she gradually came to understand how lack of consideration for her legitimate needs as a child had affected her and had led to the subsequent development of her narcissistic personality. She began to understand that her unreasonable expectations and lack of consideration for the feelings of others had undermined many of her relationships, including her marriages. Family therapy was successful in allowing for a greater sense of mutual understanding, and more importantly, the need for boundaries and limits so that Clarissa and Jack could feel safe with her again. This resulted in Belinda's gradual reengagement and reconciliation with her family.

Belinda is an example of a moderate case of narcissism, even if her behaviors actually seemed more severe than moderate. This is because she was eventually able to achieve self-awareness about how her personality had affected her relationships, and had been able to modify her behavior accordingly. She remained fairly narcissistic in her general dealings with people, but became able to rein in her more egregious behaviors. Belinda was able to sustain a better relationship pattern with her family, albeit with much coaching and assistance during therapy. Clarissa also came to accept her mother and her limitations, but only once Belinda was able to demonstrate that she could comply with and respect her daughter's limits and boundaries, which she eventually was able to accomplish.

Severe

People with severe narcissism typically are unable to hear criticism or accept any responsibility for their interpersonal problems. They are highly defensive, and they project blame onto the people around them in order to absolve themselves of any responsibility. They are also very critical and relentlessly judgmental. People with this severe form of narcissism are not usually good therapy candidates because of their of high level of defensiveness and intolerance of any negative feedback which is a prerequisite for successful therapy. They typically have no insight and have limited ability to change.

CASE EXAMPLE 6: SAM

Sam's ex-wife, Nili, came for treatment to help her to deal with the aftermath of what she described as "the divorce from hell" which she had endured for almost five years. As a result of her ex-husband Sam's constant manipulation, reneging on previous agreements, and unending threats, she had gained a considerable amount of weight and had difficulty managing her responsibilities as a sole parent. Sam refused to participate in any parenting functions whatsoever and, in fact, made things difficult by withholding child support and frequently hauling her back to court to challenge some parental decision with which he disagreed. After years of abuse and infidelity, Nili finally mustered the courage and strength to end the marriage when she found out that Sam, a very successful surgeon, had been in a torrid affair with his office manager for over a year. Their friends and community apparently had known about the affair, which was quite humiliating for her. Sam added insult to injury by blaming her for pushing him into the affair by gaining weight over the years. He also blamed her lack of regard for his sexual needs, which included sado-masochistic sex games that she abhorred. His total lack of remorse was the last straw for Nili, on top of years of Sam humiliating her by taunting her about her weight. In fact, her endocrinologist diagnosed her weight gain as the result of severe hypothyroidism and diminished metabolic functioning, which the doctor attributed to the endless stress of her very toxic marriage.

Sam's father, a Vietnam War veteran, had been extremely abusive to him, especially when he tried to assert himself as an emerging adolescent. Any attempt to make autonomous decisions, or to express an interest in anything but "tough guy" activities such as guns or boxing, his father's favorite pastime activities, were met with contempt and ridicule. His mother was powerless and easily intimidated. She did nothing to intervene, and would often mumble, "Well, you know how your father is, Sam." He gradually came to hate her even more than his father, and then he generalized that hatred to women in general. Sam's first sexual experiences ended rather quickly because he liked rough sex. Later, he came to seek out prostitutes who would agree to engage in S&M activities.

Sam's relationship with his two sons mirrored his relationship with his own father, as he ridiculed their weaknesses and showed only contempt for their lack of athleticism and their interest in activities such as computers and card games. They despised him, and he showed no interest or effort in engaging them in any type of relationship. He fought relentlessly in court over custody and, eventually, unreasonable visitation rights, only to ignore them once the battles were over. Any attempts to enter therapy during the marriage or to mediate the divorce ended abruptly due to his contempt for authority figures who were all "imbeciles." He engaged in endless sabotage of any efforts to remediate his situation. When I called him and asked him if he would be willing to meet with me to discuss how he and his ex-wife could work together and function better as parents to their children, he told me that he had better things to do with his time and money, and promptly hung up on me.

Sam is a prime example of a person with severe Narcissistic Personality Disorder. He is abusive and malevolent in his relationships, shows no remorse, and is incapable of any insight into the dynamics of his personality or how malignant his impact is on others. He projects blame, holds others responsible for his failings and refuses to compromise or work collaboratively when he feels that he has been victimized. He blamed Nili for initiating the divorce, and was indelibly wounded by the perceived rejection, even though it was his abuse and unabashed infidelity that gave her no choice but to end the marriage.

Severe narcissists are generally incapable of real intimacy or stable relationships, unless they are in complete control of a willing partner. They generally resist therapy, and they don't usually change over the course of their lifetime. They usually project the blame for the relationship difficulties on their spouses and can't acknowledge any responsibility at all for the breakdown of a relationship. Many marry and divorce several times, thinking that the real problem is that they just couldn't find the right partner to meet their needs.

Pervasiveness

The concept of pervasiveness relates to the extent to which narcissistic behavior or thinking permeates one's personality and interpersonal functioning. Some people can be extremely narcissistic with, for example, their spouse or children, but somehow come across as generous or even altruistic in relationships outside of their families. For others, the opposite is true. They can be ruthlessly aggressive, abusive, or otherwise malevolent in their business or professional life, but are totally different with their own families. Others are self-centered, critical, or insensitive with just about everyone, at work, at home, or with friends—that's just who they are.

This is an important descriptor variable, because pervasiveness relates to changeability. People who can be kind or altruistic in some aspects of their lives tend to have a greater ability to modify their narcissistic behaviors in the other aspects where self-centeredness does emerge, because they "have it in them" at some level. They seem to have the capacity to be other-centered and accepting of others, even if this ability does not generalize to all of their relationships. Therefore, these individuals may have a greater ability to improve all of their interpersonal relations if they can learn to apply or implement their "good side" in their most challenging relationships.

CASE EXAMPLE 7: LARRY

Larry's relationship with his mother Ruthie has always been close and protective. She was widowed at an early age, so she and her son went through life together with a close bond of mutual protectiveness. When Larry married Sandy, the relationship between the two women was rocky from the start. Ruthie resented Sandy's intrusion into their "special" relationship, and Sandy resented the overly close bond between Larry and his mother. Since Larry was always the center of Ruthie's world, and she made every effort to make sure that he realized how special he was, it was only natural for him to develop a sense about himself as the center of his world, and to expect to be treated as such. Although at first Sandy appreciated the respect and support that Larry showed his mother, she rather quickly felt the need to moderate the enmeshment that was obviously a prominent feature of the relationship. Instead of understanding Sandy's need to help him strike a healthy balance between his relationship with his mother and their marriage, Larry resented her intrusion and what he perceived as her jealousy toward his mother. He resisted all attempts to change how he dealt with Ruthie. Therefore, he insisted on answering her calls, at any time of the day or night, even during intimacy. He demanded that Ruthie be included at most dinners with little respite for Sandy. He resented her criticism of his mother and the way she treated her, and was uncomfortable being, for the first time, the object of such negativity, since Ruthie only praised and coddled him.

Eventually, Larry became more critical and sullen toward Sandy, playing the role of a victim of her cruel attempts at distancing and punishing his poor mother. He became passive-aggressive, ignoring or "forgetting" her requests for basic emotional or relationship needs, such as being home on time for dinner, helping her clear the table, or setting aside time to talk or to go out, as he had promised countless times. Eventually, they came in for marital therapy to deal with these issues, including his insensitive and hurtful behavior toward her.

What hurt her most was his ability to be so kind and thoughtful, not only to his mother, but to other relatives, friends, and even his accounting clients. It seemed that everyone loved him, but his narcissism threatened the viability of his marriage. Eventually, through therapy, Larry was able to see that his relationship with his mother, and its lack of boundaries, was inappropriate and indeed threatening to his marriage. He was gradually able to modulate the intensity of his connection with his mother, and to show the same benevolence to Sandy that he demonstrated in his other relationships.

The story of Larry and Sandy is an example of how the issue of prevalence is a critical factor in assessing the relative impact of narcissism and in the eventual outcome of an intervention to modify it. Because Larry had the clear ability to be loving and thoughtful in his other relationships, it was easier for him to become so with his wife. This was particularly true once he was able to understand that Sandy's efforts to modify the intensity of his closeness with Ruthie was really for the good of the marriage, and not because she was being selfish or jealous. Larry's overprotectiveness of his mother resulted from their unique experiences as a single mother and son going through life alone. Ruthie also became overly dependent on him, making him a parentified child. This need to take care of his mother at all costs persisted even when he married since he made no modifications to accommodate the needs of a new wife and a growing family. Once he became aware of these dynamics, and the need for modification, the narcissism receded rather rapidly. The loving side of Larry reemerged fairly effortlessly, and the marriage gradually rebounded and eventually flourished.

Frequency

Frequency refers to the extent that narcissistic behavior or thinking is evident in relationships. How often an individual demonstrates narcissistic behavior depends on a number of things, including the dynamics of a particular relationship, baggage, triggers, mood, impulse control, and maturity. People in toxic relationships that tend to trigger the baggage from their past—especially if they aren't emotionally mature or stable—demonstrate narcissism more frequently than those who are more personally contained and who can, therefore, better contain the narcissistic aspects of their personalities.

CASE EXAMPLE 8: JERRY AND EVA

Jerry and Eva were both children of Holocaust survivors. Their parents were victims of unspeakable horrors during their younger years. Jerry's parents were scarred by the loss of their own parents at an early age, and they were left to fend for themselves in ghettos and concentrations camps, damaging their ability to respond to the needs of their children. Jerry grew up in a home that was traumatizing, in terms of his parents' strong emotional reactions, and sparse, in terms of his parents' ability to nurture him or to build him up as a person. Consequently, he grew into an angry, resentful, critical person who constantly put others down, or complained about how others treated him poorly. It was as if Jerry had absorbed his parents' persecution complexes in a very real way.

Eva grew up in the same social circle as Jerry, and shared the same family history as a child of a survivor. She married him because she was already in her late 20s and was under intense pressure to find a husband and start a family. Her parents were less scarred than Jerry's, and were supportive and loving toward their only daughter. As an only child, she never developed the ability or need to share, and she was somewhat selfish and self-absorbed. However, she developed good social skills, and was very much capable of sustaining healthy relationships with her cousins and her circle of friends.

The marriage was stormy from the beginning, as Jerry's emotional scars and relentless negativity took its toll on Eva. However, whereas his criticism and devaluing were constant, Eva's narcissism manifested only periodically, usually when she'd just had enough of him or when she was worn down. Only then, she would strike out with withering criticism and self-absorbed activities such as shopping sprees or costly makeovers to soothe her injured soul. Otherwise, she managed to keep things cool and calm under duress and to keep the family stable.

Jerry and Eva's story demonstrates differences in terms of frequency of narcissistic behaviors, and the relative difference of impact. Whereas Jerry's constant berating of Eva took its toll on her and the marriage, it was Eva's relatively infrequent manifestation of her narcissism, and her ability to be resilient under fire, that kept their unfortunate marriage together until their last child married. Eva filed for divorce a month later.

Situational Context

An individual's situational context also contributes to the frequency of narcissistic behavior. Some people can be very effective and successful in most of their relationships; however, if they had a particularly controlling or critical parent, for example, they may find that they react in a hypersensitive or reactive way in situations in which they feel controlled or criticized. Certain situational dynamics seem to bring out the worst in people who are otherwise positive and in control of their emotions in most situations or relationships in their lives.

CASE EXAMPLE 9: LENORE

Lenore was a successful mortgage broker who had a good marriage and family life. She was proud of her ability to manage her family and to be a loving mother to her five very active children. She was competent, organized, and appreciative of the support that her loving husband Phil gave her by being an active father and partner around the house.

Lenore grew up in a strict, controlling family, with a dominating mother who had to have absolute authority around the house. Her father was in the military, and was absent for most of her formative years, leaving her mother with free rein to rule the roost as she pleased. Lenore survived by being an active, over-achiever in school, and spending as much time as possible in after-school activities or at the homes of her friends, whenever her mother allowed it. Lenore's manager referred her for treatment because several times she reacted with rage to her direct supervisor, an older, very rigid, controlling woman. Lenore was extremely sensitive to remarks that her manager made to redirect how she dealt with certain VIP clients. This supervisor felt the need to micromanage Lenore and to interfere with her work with these clients because she wasn't conducting business the way the manager preferred, even though Lenore was still a highly successful broker. As a result, Lenore ignored her supervisor for weeks, refused to meet with her, and criticized her loudly to her fellow brokers.

Lenore's situation is a good representation of someone in a situational context that elicits regressed, narcissistic behavior, but is an otherwise stable, loving person who is successful in other relationships. Her supervisor triggered Lenore's narcissism by igniting her old baggage regarding her mother's controlling, autocratic personality. Lenore's narcissistic side didn't seem evident within the situational context of a supportive, and non-controlling spouse and loving family, but it came out in abundance within the context of a supervisor whose personality was painfully reminiscent of that of her toxic mother.

CHAPTER 5

Can I Change? Parameters of the Ability to Transform

Workability

When patients come into my office, I often do an informal assessment of their ability to work with me to achieve their goals. I do this, to some extent, to determine the extent the person will be a good therapy candidate in general or, in the case of marital or adolescent therapy, to give the spouses or parents an indication of how effective I feel I will be in working with their family member. To some degree, this is a matter of managing expectations, since particularly difficult patients present unique challenges, and it's important to be realistic about what patients and their families can expect in each individual clinical situation.

Although usually I can assess workability with a fair degree of success, prevailing wisdom says psychologists can be pretty good at explaining the past and perhaps even better at observing the present, but quite poor at predicting the future. So, any attempt to forecast who will or won't be workable—and that includes you—is often an exercise in futility. Fairly often, those who at first appear impossible to work with turn out to be signature successes, and those whom we assess as quite workable end up being the patients from hell or the ones who terminate therapy abruptly because of some imaginary injustice.

Notwithstanding that caveat, here are five factors that describe a more workable patient, someone who is more likely to be successful in achieving his or her goals through therapy:

1. **Reliable**—Has a good attitude, comes in willingly, feels positive about therapy, and expects it to be helpful.

2. **Responsible**—Comes in regularly, more or less on time, and doesn't cancel appointments capriciously.

3. **Responsive**—Takes homework assignments seriously and completes them diligently.

4. **Realistic**—Has reasonable expectations and doesn't expect to achieve his or her therapeutic goals overnight.

5. **Appreciative**—Grateful to have his or her problems addressed and eased, and able to show appreciation for the opportunity to change.

Of course, there are more factors that may influence a patient's workability, but in general I have found these five most predictive of a successful therapeutic outcome.

Changeability

Similar to workability in some ways, changeability is the capacity to effect real change in yourself. This is another important factor in determining how likely a patient is to have a successful experience in therapy. Like workability, changeability is a predictor variable that influences the probability that a patient will achieve his or her expected therapy goals. It is somewhat different than workability in that it specifically focuses on your ability to transform yourself into the person you strive to become.

You can achieve some behavioral goals in therapy without experiencing real change in yourself as a person. The ability to undergo a true transformation of the inner self, to change your personality construct, is a much higher form of self-actualization, which you can assess in terms of changeability. The word "transform" refers to the fundamental conversion to becoming a different person who not only no longer demonstrates previous behavioral or emotional symptoms, but who now has integrated new perspectives, thought and behavioral patterns. This transformation calls for making substantial changes in the ways you interact with your environment, especially in regard to relationships.

In my clinical experience over the years, I've found five factors that seem to determine someone's capacity to achieve a fundamental change of self as a result of a completed therapy experience:

1. **Motivation**—A person obviously has to have some level of motivation to change in order for change to happen. Experiencing real change takes sustained effort, so without the proper level of motivation, change is not likely to occur. As the joke says, "How many psychologists does it take to change a light bulb? Only one, but the light bulb has to want to change."

2. **Intellectual Level**—Comprehending the abstract concepts we often discuss in therapy takes some level of intelligence. A patient must be able to understand subtle nuances in the complexities of human nature and interpersonal situations. Generally speaking, I find that changeability is somewhat, but not highly, correlated with intelligence, which is really more of a prerequisite than a predictor variable. Indeed, some of the least changeable patients I have seen were highly intelligent. Many, if not most, narcissists tend to be very intelligent, at least in terms of raw intellectual capacity. Often, they unfortunately just use their smarts to work against themselves by finding more intricate and convoluted ways to sabotage the therapeutic process and, consequently, their own potential for successful change. Still, patients need some degree of intelligence—intellectual, emotional, social, or otherwise—to maximize their chances of success in therapy.

3. **General Mental Health**—To experience meaningful change, you need some degree of mental health and emotional stability. This doesn't mean you have to be perfectly healthy and stable to change, but it does mean not having one of the major mental illnesses that usually deter a person's ability to experience transformative change. I'm referring

to such illnesses as schizophrenia, bipolar disorder with psychotic episodes, major depressive illness, or pervasive developmental disorders, like autism. The criteria of being mentally healthy also may exclude patients with severe, unremitting personality disorders (see Chapter 4). With such illnesses and disorders, stability or modest behavioral changes are more realistic therapeutic goals. These conditions make real transformative change far more difficult to achieve.

4. Flexibility—The ability to change is predicated on your ability to be flexible, and to respond to changes in your perceptions, insights, awareness, and personal circumstances. Flexibility refers to the ability to adapt and to respond to outside influences. The opposite of flexibility is rigidity, the inability to respond to changes in awareness or understandings that would prompt a more reasonable, flexible person to change accordingly. So, a patient may have a cognitive or intellectual understanding of the need to respond to a spouse's legitimate needs or requests, but still be unable to quite make the required behavioral changes. Such people are simply too stuck in their ways or too stubborn. People with Obsessive-Compulsive Personality Disorder (OCPD) often fit into this category, since their personality characteristics are most likely to be rigid and inflexible, and thus they find it usually difficult to modify their behavior.

5. The Ability to Be Introspective—To experience real change, it is usually not enough for patients to be intelligent, motivated, stable, and flexible. They also have to have the capacity to look inside themselves in a detached non-defensive manner, to see themselves in all of their glorious dysfunction, and to determine what they really need to do to accomplish their therapeutic goals. Some people can have all of the above characteristics, but still be so defensive, and incapable of seeing themselves honestly and objectively, that they're truly incapable of change. Narcissists are notorious for lacking introspection since they intrinsically defend themselves against the threat of revealing how truly inadequate they are as people. At this point, it's important to

differentiate between those of us who don't introspect because it is too threatening to look inward and really see who we truly are, versus those of us who intrinsically lack the capacity to introspect because of cognitive impairments or a general inability to experience real insight. Those threatened by introspection are generally capable of breaking through their narcissistic defenses and seeing themselves more clearly, perhaps with the assistance of a therapist, whereas the latter usually are stuck in the abyss of psychological nearsightedness—the inability to see within.

The concept of insight is closely related to introspection. People who can really change also have the capacity to develop a deeper understanding of what is happening in their lives. They can put the pieces together that can explain the development of their personality and how that, in turn, affected their relationships. Insight can play an important, even critical, role in healing damaged relationships. Sharing insight, along with feeling and expressing regret for the damage done, can go a long way toward rebuilding trust and safety, key ingredients in the therapeutic process of repairing relationships.

Benevolent Versus Malevolent Narcissism

Narcissists generally fall into two broad categories, benevolent or malevolent (sometimes called malignant) narcissists. Benevolent narcissists don't mean to harm other people. I sometimes refer to them as Mister Magoo, referring to the 1960s cartoon character who was nearly blind, and kept running into people, mistakenly causing all kinds of mischief, but having no clue about how much damage he was causing. Mister Magoo was kind of a loveable guy, who was pretty benign despite the swath of destruction he caused in his dealings with the people in his life. Similarly, benevolent narcissists can be well intended, generous, and likeable, but they're often clueless about the needs of their spouses or children, insensitive to the feelings of others, and otherwise self-absorbed and self-involved. They're happy to help you out or do you a favor, as long as it doesn't conflict with their favorite TV show or their favorite team's football game. In that case, forget about relying on them for help, because they're usually incapable of putting others' needs in front of their own, at least not without a lot of help along the way.

However, benevolent narcissists are often more capable of real change because they are fundamentally good people, and they often have the best of intentions. They don't want to hurt their spouses or alienate their children. Indeed, they often have an essential need to be liked or admired, and they seek approval of people around them. They simply aren't aware, or aren't other-aware; they don't see the needs, feelings, or sensitivities of the people in their lives and they are blind to what's really going on inside themselves. They don't know what they need to change in order to be effective in their relationships. Once they're aware, and become attuned to what the other person is experiencing, they're capable of true empathy. They can feel—or at least understand at some level—what the other person is feeling.

With the proper motivation, having the other prerequisites to change noted above, and having a therapist who understands narcissism and has experience working with narcissists, a benevolent narcissist can definitely change, and develop into a more interpersonally attuned, effective person.

Malevolent narcissists, on the other hand, are generally not good people at all. Their form of narcissism is more of a character disorder. It manifests as abusive behavior, including attempts at dominating, controlling, criticizing, and devaluing other people, and intentionally causing them harm. Malignant narcissists often are sociopathic, as well, which means they exploit and abuse others with no remorse. Some actually enjoy causing others pain and humiliation, and can be borderline sadistic in their behaviors and attitudes toward others. Malevolent or malignant narcissists usually aren't motivated to change at all and often lack the ability. This pessimistic outlook about malevolent narcissists is not unrealistic or overly dramatic. A true malignant narcissistic is someone whom you can only avoid or excise from your life.

Motivation to Change

The good news is that if you buy this book and, especially if you've gotten this far, chances are excellent that you're not a malevolent narcissist. Such narcissists typically can't change and don't have the desire to change for the benefit of another person. So if you're still reading, you're likely to have the benevolence that allows you to work on changing for the benefit of your spouse or because you want to have a better relationship with your alienated children, or become a better mother or father. You really don't mean to harm anyone, although you may have a strained or broken relationship with your parents, or your siblings, or you can't keep a friend or a job. You're just clueless as to why you can't seem to make a relationship work. So, be confident that, in all probability, you have the type of narcissism that is capable of and conducive to real, transformative change. You only have to be willing to do the work to make it happen.

Motivation can be extrinsic or intrinsic, or perhaps a little of both. Extrinsic motivators come from outside of yourself, such as the need to avoid a divorce, or as in the case of Belinda in Chapter 4, the need to reconcile with alienated adult children. Extrinsic motivation can also come from the need to get or keep a job. Perhaps your supervisor asked you to get help because you've alienated your co-workers or because he doesn't want to deal with you anymore. Finally, extrinsic motivation can come from the realization that you will not achieve your goals in your life, financial or otherwise, at the rate that you are going, because your personality, behaviors, and attitudes toward others have kept you from being the successful person you really want to be.

Intrinsic motivation comes from within. It comes from realizing that you're not satisfied with the level of intimacy in your life, or with your ability to attain and maintain quality relationships, or achieve real happiness. Narcissists are typically unhappy at some level, and you may be sick of being miserable. You may also realize that becoming a career victim, chronically projecting blame onto others, failing to take responsibility for your mistakes, has caused you nothing but misery and failure. People who are intrinsically motivated to change have achieved a higher degree of awareness and insight into what's really happening in their lives. The fog of denial, defensiveness, and distortion has cleared, and now they can see the reality of their personalities and their lives more clearly. Intrinsic motivation gives far greater and deeper meaning to the effort to change. The goal isn't just to be more successful; it's to have a more meaningful and productive life as a whole, leading to higher levels of self-awareness, self-actualization, and life satisfaction.

Prognostic Considerations

The term "prognosis" refers to the extent to which you can expect to achieve healing, personal transformation, and the achievement of your therapeutic goals. When a clinician takes on a patient, the therapist generally formulates an early prognosis that influences whether to take the patient, what the patient's realistic expectations should be, and the extent to which the patient can achieve his or her established therapeutic goals.

All of the factors discussed so far in this chapter are prognostic considerations. Generally speaking, if you are a workable patient who has the right attitude coming in, and you're reliable, responsible, responsive, realistic, and appreciative, your prognosis will be more positive. The more changeable you are, that is, if you are motivated, intelligent, emotionally stable, flexible, and introspective, your prognosis just jumped up a couple of notches. This is especially so if you are more of a benevolent, rather than a malevolent, narcissist. And finally, if your motivation is more intrinsic than extrinsic, you are well on your way to a complete transformation out of the world of narcissism and into the world of interpersonal success.

Self-Rating of Prognosis for Recovery from Narcissism

Instructions: Rate yourself, as honestly as possible, in terms of the items below, on a scale from 0 to 5. Add the scores, and then compare them to the rating system at the bottom of the scale. To make life more interesting, ask your spouse or partner to rate you separately, and then compare your score with that of your partner. This may prove to be an illuminating exercise in terms of your sense of objective reality.

WORKABILITY						
	0	1	2	3	4	5
Attitude (Willingness)						_____
Responsible (Appointments)						_____
Responsive (Assignments)						_____
Realistic (Goals)						_____
Appreciative						_____
TOTAL WORKABILITY SCORE (0–25)						_____

CHANGEABILITY						
	0	1	2	3	4	5
Motivation						_____
Intelligence						_____
Stability						_____
Flexibility						_____
Introspection						_____
TOTAL CHANGEABILITY SCORE (0–25)						_____
Benevolent (0) vs Malevolent (5)						_____
Intrinsic (0) vs Extrinsic (5) Motivation						_____
TOTAL SCORE (0–60)						_____

SCALE: *50–60: Excellent prognosis*   ***30–40:*** *Fair prognosis*
        40–50: Good prognosis   ***Below 30:*** *Poor prognosis*

Epigenetics

The concept of epigenetics has recently emerged in the psychological world. Briefly, it refers to our ability to modify or transform ourselves beyond our genetic predispositions. Contrary to Darwinian philosophy that our genes dictate our destiny, epigenetics (literally "above the genes") suggests that we have the capacity to transcend our genetic realities, and modify ourselves in ways that better conform with our personal goals.

The first documented example of epigenetics affecting behavior was provided by a study at McGill University in Montréal in 2004, which discovered that the type and amount of nurturing a mother rat provided in the early weeks of a baby rat's infancy determines how that rat responds to stress later in life. Researchers observed actual changes in the rats' DNA structure since their birth as a result of the mothers' heightened nurturing. This was the first time scientists documented a change in DNA as a result of early parenting experiences, as opposed to a particular genetic profile.

Later studies found that the DNA of identical twins who were separated at birth had changed in relation to anxiety and risk-taking. Given different upbringings in very different environments, the twins had developed DNA markers that obviously weren't present when they were born. Identical twins, by definition, have identical DNA, so any variations in DNA structure later in life are likely due to epigenetic changes as a result of environmental influences.

The implication of epigenetics is that we are not bound by our family histories, genetic makeup, or biologically based disorders that lock us into always being who we are today. To the contrary, it suggests that you are free to break out of your genetic framework and—through the journey of having therapy, changing your environment, modifying the friends with whom you interact, altering your thought patterns, and learning new relationship skills—you can absolutely change your personality, and become more of the person you want to be.

CHAPTER 6

Is That All There Is?
Coexisting Conditions That Can Make Things Complicated

Co-Morbidity

Nothing in life is simple, and that's certainly the case in psychology in general, and specifically with regard to personality. Some people present with only narcissism as the predominant feature of their personality and psychological profile, whereas many others appear to be more complex, having other coexisting conditions that manifest independently within their own framework or that interact perniciously with narcissism. This can potentiate or exacerbate the condition, making it much more difficult to change your life and improve your relationships. Co-morbidity refers to a situation in which a person has different types of pathology ("morbidity"), and it typically makes things less straightforward and much more complicated to treat. Research seems to indicate that co-morbidity is actually more often the case than a single, uni-dimensional diagnosis of narcissism.

Let's look at several categories of disorders that are most likely to coexist with and/or interact with a narcissistic personality, including mood disorders, anxiety disorders, other personality disorders, addictions, and a variety of other psychological issues that tend to occur along with narcissism.

Mood Disorders

Many, if not most narcissists aren't happy people. Their hypersensitivity to criticism and perceived slights, their tendency to focus on being a victim, and their omnipresent relationship problems, as well as their constant, insatiable need for attention and admiration all contribute to a general lack of personal satisfaction and happiness. Additionally, the frequent need to criticize others and focus on their faults often leads narcissists to feel that life has cheated them out of what they are entitled to have—the best spouse, perfect kids, a job that always meets their needs, and the like. When they become disappointed with the people in their lives, as they invariably do, they are miserable with their lot, and they convince themselves that they will never get what they truly deserve. Finally, the self-aggrandizement and grandiosity often associated with narcissism can generate hopes for fame and fortune. When those hopes are dashed, reality can lead to profound disappointment and dissatisfaction.

Over time, this can lead to depression, since people eventually build an internal, general expectation that they will never get what they want, and that they have no hope for true happiness or the attainment of their lofty goals. However, the relationship between depression and narcissism apparently can go both ways. In some cases, the dynamics of narcissism can and often do lead to depression, as the negativity and resentment that results from the dynamics outlined above create a generalized bitter and pessimistic view of the world and of life itself. However, people who develop depression can also become narcissistic over time, since the self-absorption and victimization often associated with depression may coalesce into a more pervasive self-centeredness. Depressives can come to perceive themselves as the victim of all of the hurts and wounds heaped upon them over a lifetime, yet they may feel no personal responsibility for causing or contributing to their problems. Their constant need to focus on what's wrong and on how miserable they are, regardless of the negative impact on those around them, is a manifestation of their lack of interpersonal awareness. Their inability to see the negative impact they have on others is often a trademark of narcissism. Thus, depressed people can develop narcissistic personalities, even if they weren't necessarily narcissistic early in their lives.

Another type of mood disorder is often seen in conjunction with narcissism. The diagnostic term for this disorder is dysthymia, and it's characterized by the symptoms of chronic, low-grade depression. More significantly, it is clinically experienced as a depressive personality; the dysthymic individual is persistently negative, pessimistic, and depleted of energy. Their cup is half-empty, and much of life is gray and gloomy. Dysthymia and narcissism often go together, in that many narcissists tend to see the world in terms of what's wrong with the people around them, and what's missing from their life that they feel they deserve to have. They are often resentful, bitter, and quick to point out that they're victims of circumstances beyond their control. They are never responsible if something goes wrong; rather, they tend to project blame onto others. This negative attitude, which characterizes this type of narcissism, often intermingles with the negativity of dysthymia, leading to a more intensified version of one or the other disorder or, as is often the case, both.

Finally, we must look at bipolar disorder, once commonly known as manic-depression and characterized by severe mood instability and emotional intensity, as well as, in some cases, psychotic thinking or behaviors. Although bipolar disorder is not necessarily correlated with narcissism, per se, they can be connected. People who experience the devastating effects of bipolar disorder, especially at the extreme level, often suffer severely low self-esteem as a result of being aware of their disturbing behaviors, and the social, occupational, and legal ramifications that often result from public exposure. Although many of the bipolar patients I've seen over the years were perfectly normal and emotionally stable when not manic or depressed, others have become more hypersensitive, defensive, and difficult to work with because narcissism has seeped into their personalities as a result of their experiences. Since narcissism is a defense mechanism that shields people from facing their flaws or shortcomings, its occasional occurrence in people with bipolar disorder is not surprising, especially with those whose manic episodes or depressive reactions have caused them considerable shame or humiliation.

CASE EXAMPLE 10: WADE

Wade, a man in his late 50s, was raised in a home dominated by his father, who grew up in the Great Depression and suffered extreme poverty in his native Midwest. His father coped with the effects of his early deprivation by abusing alcohol and imposing harsh restrictions on any non-essential spending to ensure that he would never again run out of money, even though he did well as a banker and investor. He controlled everyone in the family, especially Wade's mother, who was afraid of triggering him, and would often cry in front of Wade. He saw his mother as weak and annoying, and disdained his father for being so difficult and stingy. Wade hated being in his home, and always tried to spend time in the homes of his classmates, most of whom grew tired of his bad attitude and cantankerous behavior.

As a result of his childhood experiences, Wade grew into a somber, negativistic man. He inherited a great deal of money when his father died, but he was still highly critical of his wife whenever she bought things he deemed unnecessary. His wife was a caring, emotionally driven woman. She was generous and thoughtful, traits Wade perceived as irresponsible and reckless. He had alienated his children, as well as his wife, who threatened him with a divorce if he didn't make real efforts to change his ways of dealing with the family. Through therapy, Wade began to develop an understanding of how his underlying depression (dysthymia) and his strong narcissistic traits had converged into a personality that made living with him difficult for his wife and kids.

He started to become more aware that, in the eyes of his family, he had turned into a critical, controlling man, so overly preoccupied with financial security and frugality that he had completely lost perspective, as well as their love and respect. He found it painful to realize that, in many ways, he had become a lot like his father, but with that understanding, he slowly evolved into a more self-aware, flexible, and respectful husband and father, who eventually regained the respect and affection of his family.

Anxiety Disorders

Similar to mood disorders, anxiety disorders can be associated with narcissism. Individuals who are so anxious that it undermines normal functioning also lose their self-esteem. People who suffer panic attacks, phobias, generalized anxiety, or Obsessive-Compulsive Personality Disorder (all characterized by excessive worrying, nervousness, insecurity and high anxiety for reasons not always based in objective reality) eventually can reach the conclusion that they are inferior, weak, ineffective, or abnormal. Internalizing these feelings may undermine their sense of self so much that it destroys their self-esteem. Some of these individuals develop narcissistic tendencies to defend or deflect these anxiety-related deficiencies. They artificially inflate their self-perception to compensate for weakened egos damaged by their disorders.

Psychotherapy, prudent use of anti-anxiety medications, and relaxation training can all be helpful in alleviating anxiety. Relaxation training teaches people to control their sympathetic nervous system, which governs the fight-flight-or-freeze response that kicks in when you're threatened. It tends to be overactive and more reactive in people with anxiety disorders. The goal of treatment is to strengthen the parasympathetic nervous system, that part of the body that triggers the relaxation response, and allows people to experience greater emotional control and balance.

This is especially important for those struggling with narcissism, because it enables them to process their emotions more effectively by slowing down the sympathetic nervous system. It helps to activate the left brain, the processing part of the nervous system, to enable patients to become more effective in working through insults or threats to their egos that can trigger narcissistic reactions. With relaxation therapy, people gain the opportunity to be more in control of their emotions in general, contributing to healing the damaged ego, and building higher levels of self-esteem and self-mastery.

CASE EXAMPLE 11: JARED

Jared was a 28-year-old married man, whose OCD had plagued him for most of his life. He came from a family with a history of anxiety and compulsivity. Jared had an inordinate need for things to be in order around the house and for things to be done the right way, usually his way. All surfaces had to be spotlessly cleaned every day with disinfectant, including doorknobs and counter tops, because of his paralyzing fear of infection. The pantry, spice cabinet, linen closet, and broom closet had to be meticulously organized, and he needed to ritually check all these areas to be sure they were in order. The real problem with all of this is that he expected his wife to perform all these functions as part of her domestic duties, since he worked long hours on his internet sales business. Jared also spent an inordinate amount of time on his phone, checking his competitors' pricing and deals, to the point that he often fell asleep at night on the couch, exhausted from checking other websites until the early hours of the morning.

Jared's unreasonable demands, which emanated from his OCD–related anxiety, had a profoundly negative effect on his marriage. His wife Nicole resented the burden that his disorder placed on her, especially since Jared made no effort to assist her in achieving the level of order and cleanliness that he required. She insisted that he get help for his OCD, because she had no intention of continuing to be a slave to his disorder for the rest of her life, especially since he felt entitled to having her handle all its ramifications with no help from him. Only when Nicole threatened to leave him and the members of his men's group confronted him about his unreasonable expectations and narcissistic attitude, did he begin to take her needs seriously. He agreed to a trial of SSRI medication (selective serotonin reuptake inhibitor) called Lexapro, which did reduce the intensity of his compulsivity and need for order and cleanliness, and he started therapy. In time, he began to be more helpful around the house, as he gained insight into the harmful effects of his narcissistic behaviors.

Post-Traumatic Stress Disorder

Often, some sort of trauma or, more usually, a pattern of thematically related traumas, appears in the personal history of narcissistic people. The kind of traumatic developmental wounds that contribute to the development of narcissism stays in the nervous system, raw and unprocessed. The trauma affects the brain and its ability to process the experience in a way that people normally process their experiences (more of this in Chapter 15).

Significantly, the symptoms most often associated with Post-Traumatic Stress Disorder (PTSD), such as overreactivity to trigger events and startle response, are often disguised as hyperemotionality, or just having an "anger problem." However, doctors often don't detect or diagnose the underlying PTSD dynamic. The emotional reactivity and dysregulation often seen in narcissistic personalities could, in fact, be symptoms of PTSD.

As we will discuss in the next section, different types of therapies can be extremely helpful in calming the nervous system in general, or desensitizing specific traumatic experiences that lie dormant within your nervous system, ready to be activated when you experience something similar to or associated with the earlier trauma. Healing the underlying PTSD, especially when it involves reprocessing the trauma in a way you can emotionally accept, can also help to heal the narcissism in your personality. For instance, a narcissistic man who was abused as a child can learn that the abuse wasn't due to his innate worthlessness, but was a result of the serious emotional problems of those who abused him.

Addictions

Addictions can develop to a number of temptations, including drugs, alcohol, sex, food, gambling, spending, and shopping. The general dynamic that usually underlies an addiction involves some type of trauma, history of abuse, or emotional wounding that causes addicts to try to escape their internal pain and to anesthetize themselves by acting out in a way that prevents them from experiencing their underlying painful emotions. The cycle of addiction occurs when addicts feel the backlash of the consequences of their behavior, the shame of the ramifications, and then feel the need to escape even more. So, they act out again. Alternatively, addicts report that they use substances or behave badly in other ways because they feel boredom or deep emptiness. Indulged or overprivileged individuals who are deprived of the benefits of responsibility and hard work can fail to develop the inner core necessary for developing a healthy sense of self. They often indulge in addictive behaviors because they are bored with leading unfulfilled, meaningless, empty lives. They self-stimulate to artificially fill the void.

Narcissism is often associated with addiction in several ways. First, like narcissism, addictions often result from painful or traumatic experiences that caused a breakdown of confidence and self-esteem. Narcissism and addictions are both defenses against feeling underlying pain and shame, efforts to detach from the true inner self. Addicts invariably rely on a sense of entitlement to perpetuate their addictions, convincing themselves that they have the "right" to betray their spouse with another sex partner because of the stress of their marriage, or that they "deserve" to spend an outrageous amount of money on an unneeded luxury item because they work so hard, even though they can't afford it. Entitlement is a common trademark of narcissism; the inflated ego often found in narcissists can maintain and perpetuate addictive behaviors.

Narcissism also shows up in the denial and minimization addicts often use to defend against efforts to force them to face their addiction and accept responsibility for the damage they've caused. This is a form of projection, or externalizing the blame, by pushing the focus back on those confronting them. Instead of looking at themselves in the mirror and acknowledging that they have a problem, addicts might blame their spouse for being too critical or not "with it," or blame their therapist for not understanding or for siding with their family. They also blame society for not accepting the "alternative" lifestyle that allows promiscuity, liberal use of psychoactive drugs, or spending or gambling to the point of financial ruin.

CASE EXAMPLE 12: FRANK

Frank, a twice-divorced criminal attorney, had a long history of frequenting strip joints, hiring prostitutes, and regularly getting erotic massages. He had been engaging in these behaviors since his late teens, and coming from a wealthy family with money readily available, he was always able to maintain his expensive addiction. Frank came in for therapy with his newest girlfriend, Jeanine, who had eventually realized that she could not tolerate his pattern of acting out behaviors. She'd given him an ultimatum to either get help to overcome the addiction or she would end the relationship. At first, he resisted and focused the blame on Jeanine, claiming that she was controlling and too conventional for his taste. He told her to just "get a grip" on herself. He felt that her siblings, who all had stable marriages, were influencing her and pressuring her to break things off.

In exploring the pattern of his relationships, Frank started to relax his narcissistic defenses. He began to see that the main theme of his relationship history was his inability to understand his impact on his partners, and that his criticism and projection of blame in the face of any conflict often contributed to the breakup of each relationship. More specifically, he started to realize that his lack of understanding and his gross insensitivity to his partners' feelings about his sexual acting out had led to resentment and alienation. He was eventually able to accept that the problem might, in fact, lie within him, and that his lack of empathy toward Jeanine was at the root of the problem. He saw that her unwillingness to accept his lack of awareness and his infidelities would be the case with most women. Over time, Frank was able learn the art of empathy, and to accept responsibility for the problems in the relationship. He eventually entered a 12-step program for sex addiction. A year later, Frank and Jeanine married, and he continues to work hard on his recovery, as well as on keeping the dynamics of his narcissistic personality in check.

Attention Deficit Disorder

People who grew up attached to an often-stigmatizing label such as Attention Deficit Disorder (ADD) or Attention Deficit Hyperactivity Disorder (ADHD) are usually plagued with such challenges as impulsivity, distractibility, difficulty with completing tasks, poor academic achievement, emotional reactivity, and anger management problems. The western world, with its heavy emphasis on achievement and structure, does not work well with people who have this type of profile. Schools label kids who don't conform with uniform, in-the-box expectations as problem children, underachievers, or just "bad kids." They often end up being kicked out of schools or being sent to therapists at an early age. These children get the message that the way they are is inadequate and unacceptable, which often leads to a damaged sense of self. These dynamics are fertile ground for the narcissistic defense of deflecting away feelings of inadequacy and rejection. Adults who grew up under these circumstances often protect their damaged sense of self by overcompensating, thereby fueling the grandiosity and need for material success so often associated with narcissism.

Some of the most financially successful patients whom I've seen over the years were also some of the most narcissistic as well, and many of them had been diagnosed with ADHD as children. It's no wonder. Progressive psychologists who specialize in ADHD today often conceptualize it as an alternative way of functioning, rather than as a deficit. Dr. Lynn Weiss, a clinical psychologist who has learned a lot about ADHD through her own struggles (and impressive accomplishments) as a result of having the disorder, conceptualizes it as a manifestation of a highly intelligent, creative brain. This often enables someone to think "out of the box" in a way that normally doesn't occur.

Her book, *ADD and Creativity*, expanded my thinking on the topic by broadening the concept of ADD to include those with highly creative, unconventional, but potentially successful individuals. Think President Bill Clinton—brilliant Rhodes scholar, highly effective politician, extraordinary people person—and yet, widely known as an impulsive man who too often exercised poor judgment and, probably most notoriously, was a self-indulgent, manipulative womanizer. So, here we have a classic narcissism (including a childhood of abuse) and ADHD profile—smart, creative, out-of-the-box thinker, and at the same time, clear entitlement issues, grandiosity, distortion, and projection of blame ("I did not have sex with that woman!").

Adults with ADHD can overcome the deficits associated with the disorder through interventions such as individual and group psychotherapy, and stimulant medications such as Ritalin, Adderall, and Vyvanse, all of which stimulate the frontal lobes of the brain. These areas regulate the executive functions of the nervous system, important abilities such as attention, concentration, focusing, time and space management, and task completion, all of which ADHD affects.

In addition, an experienced, well-trained ADHD or organizational coach, or an occupational therapist who specializes in ADHD, can help people track their tasks and projects and teach them organizational skills. The therapist can become a source of accountability who invaluably helps a person achieve a much higher degree of functionality. These resources can help a person be more effective and achieve goals, thus helping to heal the wounded ego, and moderate the severity of the accompanying narcissism. Therapy can alleviate the need to defend against the underlying sense of inadequacy and deficiency brought about by the deficits associated with ADHD.

CASE EXAMPLE 13: LON

Lon was a high-powered real estate developer whose sharp business acumen, wildly creative ideas, and relentless energy had brought him much financial success. However, his frequent impulsive outbursts and relentless criticism of his sons had affected his relationships with his entire family, including his wife, Susan, his sons Jeremy and Scott, and his parents. Lon grew up in an affluent eastern Long Island home, with a fiercely competitive, highly critical father—a highly regarded criminal attorney who thought Lon never measured up to him. Material possessions were a highly valued goal in his family, and he constantly compared his acquisitions to those of his own siblings. Lon grew up challenged academically, and struggled both in his studies and his behavior, whereas his brothers and sister were high-achievers with top professional accomplishments. Lon's ADHD was not diagnosed until he was an adult, because his parents saw him only as a spoiled, lazy kid, and were, quite frankly, too busy with their own careers to take the time to have him properly evaluated. Instead, they relied on their nanny and the school's counselors and tutors to make sure that Lon passed.

Lon's 15-year-old son Jeremy was the initial focus of treatment, because of his anger issues and—most importantly to his parents—because he'd been caught smoking marijuana on school grounds. It was readily apparent to me that serious family issues were involved. I asked Lon to come meet with me. At first, he refused, telling Susan, "I just want Jeremy to get fixed, not me." When she pushed, he came in reluctantly, and became belligerent when I suggested that Jeremy was harboring feelings of anger toward him. He shot back at me that he was "tired of all of the bulls—t excuses," and that all Jeremy needs is a "swift kick in the butt." He never returned for another session.

Eventually, Lon and Susan divorced. She and Scott managed to normalize their lives, though Jeremy developed a serious drug addiction. He spent much of his remaining high school years in drug rehabilitation programs, but that led eventually to his current success as a drug rehab counselor for troubled teens.

Lon continued to experience even more financial success, but he languished in a series of failed relationships, all of which ended because of his anger issues and general attitude of disrespect toward his female partners. He continues to live the life of a bachelor, often going out with several women at a time, initially luring them with his charm and good looks, but usually alienating them with his impulsive anger and destructive behaviors.

Oppositional Defiant Disorder

Angry, abused adolescents often may develop Oppositional Defiant Disorder, which manifests with oppositional and defiant behavior toward authority figures. People with ODD tend to be argumentative, and disrespectful of rules, laws, or societal mores. Adults generally see these kids as difficult to manage.

Adolescents with ODD often lack empathy and can't see things from any perspective other than their own. Without active treatment, these teenagers often develop a serious problem, Antisocial Personality Disorder (described in more detail in the next section). However, a pervasive underlying dynamic exists in these kids that also can develop into full-blown Narcissistic Personality Disorder, if the traits of self-centeredness, lack of empathy, and bouts of anger become entrenched in their personality. While all narcissists aren't oppositional or defiant, all ODD people are narcissistic in at least some ways, and can develop into complete narcissistic personalities if the individual is left untreated and remains in the environment that created the condition in the first place.

In terms of the formative conditions for the development of ODD, I've usually experienced parents who are overly controlling and critical, or who are in conflict themselves, and show disrespect or disdain for each other in front of their children. If kids see that the two primary authority figures in their lives blatantly disrespect each other, it's easy to understand how they can develop disrespect for authority and a blatant disregard for limits and rules in general.

Personality Disorders

The world of psychiatric diagnosis has two general diagnostic classifications. "Axis I" incorporates all the psychiatric disorders mentioned heretofore, as well as many other psychiatric conditions commonly referred to as "mental disorders." "Axis II" encompasses what are referred to as "personality disorders." Generally speaking, personality can be defined as a "relatively enduring, defined pattern of interacting with one's environment." As such, personality is a sort of template of interpersonal relations. The field then defines a personality disorder as a maladaptive or dysfunctional way in which individuals interact with their environment, invariably resulting in impaired relationships. The following discussion covers the personality disorders which, in my experience, are the most common ones that can coexist with a narcissistic personality.

Obsessive-Compulsive Personality Disorder

As opposed to OCD, a mental disorder which, as discussed above, involves obsessions and compulsive behaviors, Obsessive-Compulsive Personality Disorder (OCPD) is a pattern of rigidity, perfectionism, and controlling behaviors that often alienates other people. As you can imagine, controlling, rigid, perfectionistic people can be difficult to live with, and people with OCPD also often are highly critical of those around them who don't meet their unrealistic high standards, and that's usually everyone.

As opposed to OCD, in which sufferers are usually unsettled, anxious, and disturbed by their symptoms, people with OCPD are perfectly (no pun intended) fine with their perfectionist expectations and standards. When OCPD combines with narcissism, it can be especially pernicious to any relationship. The NPD/OCPD combination can be extremely toxic in relationships because it is difficult to "breathe" when you're with someone who is so pressurizing and controlling that you can lose your sense of self. When it's "my way or the highway," or everything has to be done correctly—of course, that's my way—the other person has little, if any, room for autonomous choices or behaviors, independent thinking, or self-expression. The NPD/OCPD person's absolute, black-and-white thinking makes any attempts at living more in the grey areas of life, accounting for the complexities of living, or thinking in a moderate or temperate way futile and of little consequence.

OCPD is difficult as a sole entity, but when it presents itself in combination with narcissism, the level of challenge and difficulty to anyone who must deal with the person increases exponentially. Coping with a rigid perfectionist is bad enough, but when he or she is also demanding, entitled, humiliating, defensive, and incapable of being aware of the impact of his or her expectations and behaviors, having any type of a quality, meaningful relationship is pretty impossible. It's a double whammy of sorts, as the other person not only has to deal with the stress of living up to unreasonable expectations, but also has to endure the humiliation of narcissistic criticisms that destroy his or her self-esteem, and any hope of real intimacy.

CASE EXAMPLE 14: JOE

Joe was a successful surgeon whose practice had thrived due to his orderly, meticulous methods and demands for perfection from his surgical team. Although his staff respected his high degree of expertise and standards, they also loathed him personally. He had alienated patients with his arrogant and unsympathetic bedside manner.

Larry, Joe's colleague and brother-in-law, referred him for therapy. As a doctor and as a patient in the hospital, Larry had heard that Joe had difficulty retaining office staff, and that several members of his surgical team were planning to leave for another practice that was opening up in the same hospital medical building. Larry asked to accompany Joe to his first appointment, during which he shared his observations and concerns with Joe, and suggested that he work on his personality and relationship skills to save his practice. Joe reacted at first with indignation and rage, accusing his brother-in-law of being jealous of his superior skills and status as a surgeon, since Larry was "only an internist," and lacked his highly specialized skills and expertise.

After meeting with Joe's wife, Cheryl, who corroborated Larry's impressions and concerns based on her relationships with the office staff and her familiarity with their complaints, I asked Joe if he would allow me to meet with his staff, to ascertain the validity of Cheryl and Larry's observations, and to see how I could assist him in dealing more effectively with his professional relationships.

I met individually with a few key members of his clinical team, and had a private meeting with his office staff. It was readily apparent that his practice had a serious problem, and that the staff's level of job dissatisfaction was quite high. Most reported insulting, abusive behavior, absurd and fluid performance expectations that were impossible to fulfill, and a generally rigid, tense atmosphere that had become quite stressful. It was impossible for his team to function at any level of comfort or success. Most of the staff members, I discovered, were actively looking for another position, and the threat of his practice imploding was quite real.

Working with Cheryl and Larry, we decided to have an intervention, with his office manager of 20 years, associate partner, his wife, and his head surgical nurse all in attendance. One by one, they all lovingly, but assertively reported to him about the impact of his personality and behavior on their morale and on retaining his patients. He heard from them that his employees had become demoralized and passive-aggressive, avoiding tasks that they knew Joe wanted done quickly, allowing the resentment to affect their job performance. His surgical teammates gave him feedback about the effects of his harsh criticisms and insults during surgery anytime things didn't stack up as perfectly as he had demanded. They made it clear that he could very possibly lose his entire team soon if things didn't change quickly and radically.

Joe realized then that he really had no choice but to work on himself in order to save his practice. He entered treatment to work on, not only the perfectionism and rigidity due to his OCPD, but also on his gross insensitivity and lack of awareness of his behavior's impact that resulted from his narcissism. He eventually began to try to develop humility, and to recognize and accept his own imperfections, as well as those of the people around him. His spirituality as a devout Catholic also assisted him in becoming more of a servant of G-d, rather than an arrogant monster, and, in time, he transformed himself into a more humble, calm, and respectful physician and team leader. No one in his office ended up leaving, and the atmosphere in the office—and at home—improved dramatically as a result of Joe's efforts to change.

Sociopathy/Antisocial Personality Disorder

As opposed to Joe, a highly moralistic person with a great deal of integrity despite his rather severe interpersonal flaws, sociopaths, or those who are diagnosed with what is called Antisocial Personality Disorder, tend to be amoral, manipulative, exploitive, and deceptive in their dealing with other people. They have no compunction whatsoever about lying, cheating, or taking advantage of others for personal gain or pleasure. They have no problem manipulating or abusing vulnerable people, and often have absolutely no remorse for the damage that they have caused. In fact, they often enjoy wreaking havoc. Perpetrators of child sexual abuse often have this type of personality combination, since the sexual abuse of children often involves a very calculated, deliberate grooming process, as well as a complete, and often shocking lack of remorse about the devastating effects of this depraved behavior which invariably damages the lives of these children.

In my experience, every sociopath is a narcissist at heart, because of the factors underlying the sociopathic behavior: extreme entitlement, lack of awareness or care about the impact of one's behavior, and a general self-centered focus on meeting one's needs at the expense of others. The opposite is generally not true: Every narcissist is not a sociopath. As mentioned in Chapter 4, there is a concept of benign or benevolent narcissism, in which the individuals are basically well-intended, but have an impaired ability to see beyond themselves or to be aware of their interpersonal impact. However, generally speaking, and in terms of understanding the dynamics of sociopathy, one can assume that when there's sociopathy, there's narcissism.

CASE EXAMPLE 15: JACK

Jack was a hedge fund manager who was convicted of bank fraud a few years ago. He came in for treatment with his wife, Lara, because she had recently found out that he had gotten involved in another illegal scheme involving real estate, and could get in trouble once more. She was deeply upset by this, because she thought he had learned his lesson by now, and because he showed no remorse over the fact that he had retraumatized her with his continued sociopathic behaviors. For his part, Jack blamed Lara for being too controlling, and for being a hypocrite, since she had no problem spending lots of money on luxury items such as expensive purses and jewelry.

During the course of therapy, it was discovered that Jack was having an affair with a very young worker in his office, and Lara filed for divorce. Instead of opting for a collaborative attorney, which Lara was advocating, Jack insisted on hiring a "shark" who would help him maneuver things in such a way that he would get away with minimal financial loss, which was all he was concerned with at the time. He showed no regard for the impact of that decision on his children, or his wife who was raising them. He eventually got caught operating his real estate scheme, and was embroiled in legal battles for years trying to stay out of prison. He got off of those charges, but he ultimately ended up in prison anyway for an unrelated tax evasion charge. He had failed to file his tax returns for five years, and he was caught lying on the one he did file earlier due to an IRS audit triggered by an anonymous call from someone in his office who knew that he had committed tax fraud.

Jack's case is a clear example of how often narcissism can develop into, and be exacerbated by, the presence of sociopathy. Character disorders such as Antisocial Personality Disorder are so often associated with NPD that it warrants some genuine introspection in terms of the extent to which this may be part of your own personality structure, at some level.

Borderline Personality Disorder

People who experience early, chronic trauma that pervades their childhood, often fail to develop into stable, integrated personalities. The traumas that they experience tend to overwhelm their young, underdeveloped brains, and their personalities tend to be more fragmented and unstable. Borderline Personality Disorder (BPD) is characterized by instability of emotions, mood, identity, and behavior. It can also be dangerous, involving self-destructive behaviors such as self-harm, cutting, and suicidal behavior. People with BPD often have very unstable relationships, alternating between over-idealizing others and devaluing or debasing them. They have severe difficulty regulating their emotions, and often distort reality and misconstrue events around them to fit their own distorted inner reality. Borderlines often shift among several fragmented ego states, or distinct personality fragments, some of which are very immature and destructive. Severe cases often end up with repeated hospitalizations, as a result of frequent suicide gestures or attempts, and can exhaust their family members and their therapists, as well.

Often, people who have BPD have at least one or some personality facets that are extremely narcissistic, having been severely wounded and damaged by the traumatic experiences that they endured. These early, younger facets are very childlike and, as such, are self-centered, impulsive, self-indulgent, and emotionally volatile. They often focus on themselves as victims, and fail to take responsibility for their actions, instead preferring to project blame onto others. Some people with BPD traits have healthier, more stable core personalities, but when triggered, react in extremely narcissistic, emotionally explosive ways before returning to their healthier, more stable baseline personalities. However, those who are full-blown borderlines spend their lives in a cauldron of instability and emotional drama that often precludes them from enjoying stable, meaningful relationships, or any sense of self-worth or life satisfaction. They end up being career victims, focusing on what other people do to hurt them, rather than on what they are doing to affect others negatively. They look very much like unstable narcissists who live unhappy lives of drama and self-pity, often living through repeated hospitalizations, multiple divorces, or a string of broken relationships.

CASE EXAMPLE 16: RACHEL

Rachel was a 30-something single woman, who was sexually abused by her father and by one of her brother's friends when she was young. Her mother committed suicide shortly after Rachel revealed the abuse to her. She felt abandoned by her mother's death, yet, at the same time, she felt responsible for it, and carried a lot of guilt and shame as a result of both the abuse and her mother's suicide.

Rachel worked as a nurse in a local hospital, but she often engaged in confrontations with doctors and fellow nurses on the floor whom she perceived as being "out to get her." She was perpetually resentful over a differential in salaries that left her underpaid compared to her peers, though her less than stellar performance reviews were the main reason her salary was lower than theirs. Her personal relationships were in shambles because of her paranoia and emotional volatility, and she had been hospitalized twice because of drug overdoses after breaking up with a boyfriend. She could only see what others were doing to cause her pain, but she couldn't see that they were, in fact, reacting to her alienating, often abusive behavior toward them. The world, as unstable as it was for her, revolved around her hurts, her pain, her needs, and her resentments. For her, nothing else existed.

Rachel's story embodies the dynamic interplay between BPD and narcissism. Her primary diagnosis was BPD, characterized by a history of severe trauma, emotional intensity and dysregulation, mood swings, paranoia, and a persistent pattern of relational dysfunction. However, her narcissism was also prominent, in that she had no awareness of her interpersonal impact, could see things only from her point of view, and was a perennial victim. No matter what she did to contribute to her negative circumstances, inevitably she always saw herself as the one who was being hurt.

CHAPTER 7

Defending the Fort: Commonly Used Defense Mechanisms

General Concept and History

The concept of a defense mechanism originates from early Freudian theory, which theorized that in order to protect the ego from being vulnerable to psychological threats, the unconscious mind develops various psychological strategies to manipulate, deny, or distort reality. This allows us to avoid anxiety, guilt, or self-recrimination from occurring in situations in which we would otherwise feel negative emotions about ourselves. It can also be viewed as ways that people distance themselves from being fully aware of unpleasant or unwanted thoughts, feelings, or behaviors.

A pioneer in the study of borderline and narcissistic personalities, Otto Kernberg, divided defense mechanisms into three categories: Primitive, Less Primitive, and Mature. Generally speaking, the more primitive the defense mechanism, the more effective it is in the short-term to accomplish the goal of protecting the individual from awareness and stress. However, these more primitive defense mechanisms are also the least effective in the long run, and also ones that carry the more serious negative consequences, in terms of effects on relationships, job effectiveness, and general functionality.

Primitive Defense Mechanisms

Primitive defense mechanisms are those that allow us to engage in regressive, potentially destructive behaviors, without feeling the angst that would normally accompany such experiences. Primitive defenses are seen as childlike and immature, and represent early stages of development which allow us to behave in ways that bring us immediate gratification of needs, desires, or emotions. These regressed behaviors occur regardless of the consequences, the impact on others, or the extent to which it violates basic moral values. For example:

Regression—This occurs in individuals whose behaviors or reactions represent a return to an earlier stage of development. When individuals utilize regression as a defense mechanism, they literally are not "acting their age." This defense mechanism enables them to act out in ways that would not to be tolerated for a person of their age.

Denial—This is the refusal to accept reality or facts, in a way that deflects away from the normal anxiety or other negative feelings that would normally be experienced if the person was in reality. People who are in denial act as if a painful event or future aversive consequence doesn't exist, thus allowing the person to engage in the behavior without the negative emotions that would otherwise normally occur.

Projection—This occurs when individuals "project" onto others what they unconsciously know or feel about themselves. They cannot accept the reality of their own flaws or failures, so they must project them onto those around them. The fragile ego cannot handle or face the truth about itself, so the only option is to accuse others of the same crime, so that there is ostensibly a deflection towards some distorted, fantasized version of the truth. The focus is what is wrong with others, as opposed to what is wrong about themselves.

Relationship to Narcissism

Because of their relatively fragile egos, narcissists frequently use primitive defense mechanisms to maintain their self-centered, critical, impulsive behavior. They are often incapable of being intellectually or emotionally honest about themselves and their interactions with others, so they have to distort reality to defend themselves against the inevitable criticism that they face because of the way they conduct themselves. Narcissists often exhibit regressive behaviors such as rage, impulsivity, and self-indulgence that often adversely affect the people in their lives, destroying marriages, and alienating children along the way. They distort reality by denying the impact of their behavior, or ignoring its consequences. Finally, instead of maturely accepting responsibility for their mistakes or damaging behavior, they project the blame onto others, refusing to face the ugly truth about themselves, and to take the steps that are necessary to repair the broken relationships that lie in their wake.

CASE EXAMPLE 17: DANIEL

Daniel has had a long-standing feud with his older brother Jonathan, who is more financially well-off, married, and socially upstanding. Daniel never married, and has had difficulty keeping lower level jobs. He has had a history of drug abuse, and blames his problems on his perception that his parents always favored Jonathan, and treated him differently. Daniel has been pathologically jealous of his brother for years, and resents his success, and how proud his parents are of him.

At a holiday meal, a violent incident occurred, in which Jonathan made a comment about a promotion that he recently got at his work that will require a great deal of travel, often to exotic places such as the Caribbean and Hawaii. Daniel made a crass comment about Jonathan taking the promotion to get away from his wife Sharon, and to be able to have "fun" whenever he wants to. It was an extremely inappropriate comment that shocked his parents, and humiliated Sharon. Jonathan reacted strongly to Daniel's rude comment by telling him that he was just jealous because he was such a loser who can't keep a job. The situation quickly escalated to the point that Daniel became enraged, turned the dining room table upside down and stormed out of the house, shouting obscenities at his family as he was leaving.

When his father called him out on his outrageous behavior the next morning, Daniel denied that he said what he was being accused of saying, instead claiming that he was just kidding, and that his comments were taken out of context. He accused his parents of deliberately distorting his words to make him look bad, because all they want to do is to protect their precious son Jonathan, and to "throw him under the bus" like they've done his entire life. He further blamed Jonathan for triggering him by bragging about his promotion at a holiday meal, and that it was entirely his fault for causing such a disruption to the family. There was nothing his father could do to get him to see how hurtful and destructive his comments were, or how his behavior had caused the family such pain. Instead, Daniel stubbornly held on to his own distorted narrative that it was he who was the victim here, of a family that continually causes him to feel badly by being the son that is put down and treated shabbily.

In order to protect his very fragile ego, Daniel had to resort to the use of several defense mechanisms that helped him to deflect away responsibility, and to avoid facing the real truth about himself, that he was actually the real provocateur here, and not the victim. He first used denial, in that he refused to see himself objectively as someone who caused his own problems and lack of achievement. Rather, he focused on his brother as the real source of all of his problems. This also involved the use of projection of the blame, as he chose to blame his family for his lack of success in life, rather than face the awful truth that he had no one else to blame but himself. Finally, he also utilized the defense mechanism of distortion, when he claimed that he never said the things that the entire family clearly heard him say, and that triggered the entire drama in the first place.

More Sophisticated Defense Mechanisms

There are other, less primitive defense mechanisms that reflect a more sophisticated level of psychological development and a more cognitively developed way of thinking. These defense mechanisms, nonetheless, are still employed to defend against the shame and guilt of inappropriate behavior, bad choices, and self-indulgence. These defense mechanisms are usually by people whose narcissism reflects a more subtle type of personality pathology, rather than the more regressive type of narcissism described in the case example above. Although these defense mechanisms are less primitive than the others described above, they are nonetheless still maladaptive and ineffective in dealing with painful feelings stemming from inappropriate reactions and behaviors. For example:

Justification—People who are narcissistic often justify their behavior by using excuses to explain why they did what they did, or to justify their inappropriate behavior. Instead of owning the fact that they made a mistake, they will come up with elaborate reasons for their behavior, which attempts to deflect away from the responsibility that they have for their destructive actions. Too often, they simply cannot admit that they are at fault. Instead, they develop justifications for their behavior, which absolves them from all responsibility.

Rationalization—A more sophisticated form of defense mechanism than justification, rationalization is used by highly intelligent people, who use their intellectual abilities to run circles around other people (and themselves) to explain away their behaviors and actions. Narcissistic people who rationalize their behavior can develop elaborate, and often bizarre ways of explaining away their manipulative schemes. Sociopaths frequently use rationalization to manipulate their way out of situations in which they are caught taking advantage or exploiting people who trusted them.

Intellectualization—When people become overwhelmed by emotions, they can, over time, separate from their emotional selves by engaging in overintellectualized thinking that helps them to disconnect from the pain inside of them. Bright, cognitively developed individuals can often use this defense to protect themselves from experiencing painful emotions by engaging in analytical thinking that keeps them from being in touch with their inner feelings. Intellectualization also helps narcissistic people with addictions maintain their indulgent or addictive behavior by intellectualizing the experience, as opposed to feeling the actual remorse or guilt that underlies their actions.

Compartmentalization—People who have strong narcissistic traits, but have healthier personality cores, often maintain their destructive behavior by compartmentalizing in their mind what their core self cannot accept or tolerate. Compartmentalization involves separating out in one's mind what they are doing that is unacceptable, so that their rational, healthier sides cannot challenge or stop the behaviors. This defense mechanism is often used by addicts, who can be prosocial, appropriate, and even altruistic in aspects of their lives, but secretly engage in destructive behaviors such as sexually acting out, gambling away the family's savings, or being abusive to their spouses or children. Compartmentalization often occurs in individuals whose personalities are fragmented into discrete ego states that are often incompatible with each other. It is seen as a "splitting off" of an unhealthy ego state that is capable of doing things that the person in their core ego state, would never even think of doing.

Reaction formation—It is not uncommon for people who have underlying issues that are seen to be unacceptable in society to publicly express the exact opposite belief or attitude, as an attempt to cover up the truth of what is happening deep inside the individual. A current example of this is the number of people who publicly espouse anti-gay sentiments and call for discrimination against gay people, who were later exposed for homosexual behavior. Reaction formation is a subconscious, and sometimes conscious attempt to deny or mask underlying feelings or behaviors, as a way to obfuscate the truth, and deceive others into believing something that is not true about the individual.

CASE EXAMPLE 18: JOEL

Joel was a middle-aged, well-respected insurance agent in a mid-sized city in the Midwest. He had a long history of relationships with wealthy clients who trusted him, and was also a man of faith and an elder in his church. A family man, he was a beloved father and grandfather, and admired by his community. Over the years, he convinced many of his clients to invest in a real estate business that he had developed on the side. It initially yielded high returns to investors. However, at some point, when he failed to pay dividend checks, it became painfully apparent that this was a Ponzi-like scheme that had fallen apart, and his clients had lost their investments.

When confronted with the scheme, Joel explained that his motive was purely to benefit his clients, and to allow him to contribute more to the church, as well as other charities that he supports. He expressed indignation that he would be accused of doing something illegal or immoral, something he was simply not capable of doing. He presented himself as a victim of circumstances, and that he was shocked and hurt that his clients would judge him so harshly now, when they once lauded him with praise when things were going well. His focus on himself as the victim allowed him to avoid facing the truth—that he violated the trust of people who had faith in him, who lost vast sums of money as a result of his selfish, manipulative scheme to defraud them. Joel eventually was convicted of grand theft and fraud, and was sentenced to ten years in prison, where he maintained his innocence and his role as the "real victim."

Adaptive Defense Mechanisms

There are other defense mechanisms that are seen as being more adaptive and mature, that can actually be goals of therapy in recovering from narcissism. Some of these are old Freudian concepts, whereas others are more recent permutations that have been incorporated into the concept of a defense mechanism. These more mature defense mechanisms allow for people who are challenged by stressful situations to cope with their challenges in ways that are more appropriate and functional. For example:

Sublimation—An old Freudian concept, sublimation involves choosing an alternate, more socially acceptable means of expressing an inner desire that would be otherwise unacceptable. The classic example is the man with homicidal impulses becoming a butcher. A more contemporary example is someone who has underlying attraction to children who raises funds to protect children from sexual abuse. He keeps away from situations that could elicit dangerous behavior by throwing himself into the safer world of fundraising to make sure that he is safe from doing any harm.

Humor—When emotionally developed people face stress, they often use humor as an adaptive tool to deal with the challenges that they face. Telling a funny story or a well-selected joke can neutralize an otherwise tense situation, or help the person put things in perspective. It enables people to "lighten up," and to diffuse the stress of people around them. "Laughter is the best medicine" is an age-old adage that applies here. Using humor as a tool to soothe and heal a triggered soul can be a very effective way of positively defending against stress and anxiety.

Compensation—Healthy, confident people recognize that they have both strengths and weaknesses, and are comfortable with their weaknesses. They use their strengths to compensate for their weaknesses, which allows them to achieve a healthy balance and positive self-concept. Narcissism most often originates from weaknesses and deficiencies that manifest in the grandiosity and arrogance usually associated with narcissism. People who use healthy compensation in their lives see things in the proper perspective, and allow for weaknesses and shortcomings to be acceptable and normal. People who are trying to overcome narcissism can use this mechanism to be more accepting, or even embracing of their weaknesses, work on improving them, and also focus on their strengths, so that their self-concept is more balanced, and their self-esteem is strengthened. This lessens the need for the narcissistic defense to be used to deflect away from underlying insecurity and a sense of inadequacy.

Assertiveness—As opposed to the aggressive behavior that is often displayed by narcissistic people, or the passive-aggressive behavior that can be the case, as well, assertiveness is the appropriate expression of feelings, wants, or needs that can lead to a healthy, more mature resolution of conflicts. Assertive people are also more confident and secure in their relationships and in their sense of self, and as such, feel much better about themselves. Those who are recovering from narcissism can help themselves to achieve their goal by moving towards the center of the continuum between the extremes of aggressiveness and passivity, and to become more confident, assertive people who have confidence in themselves and what they express in their relationships.

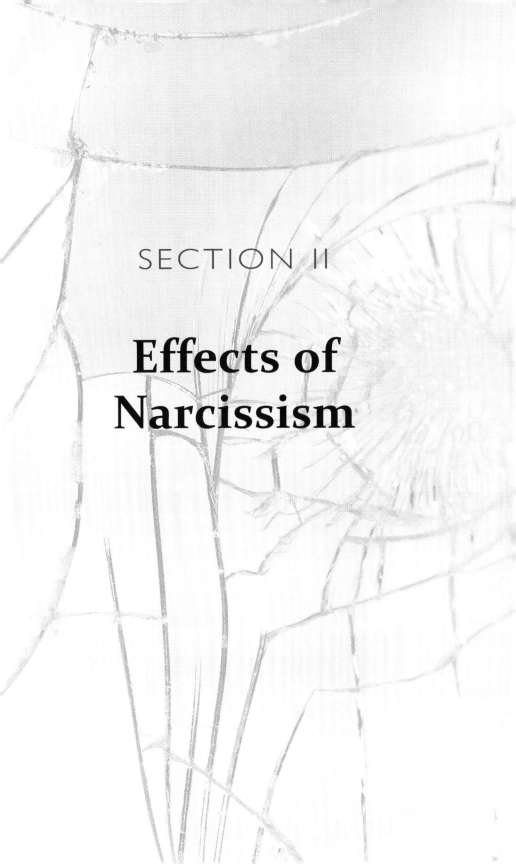

SECTION II

Effects of
Narcissism

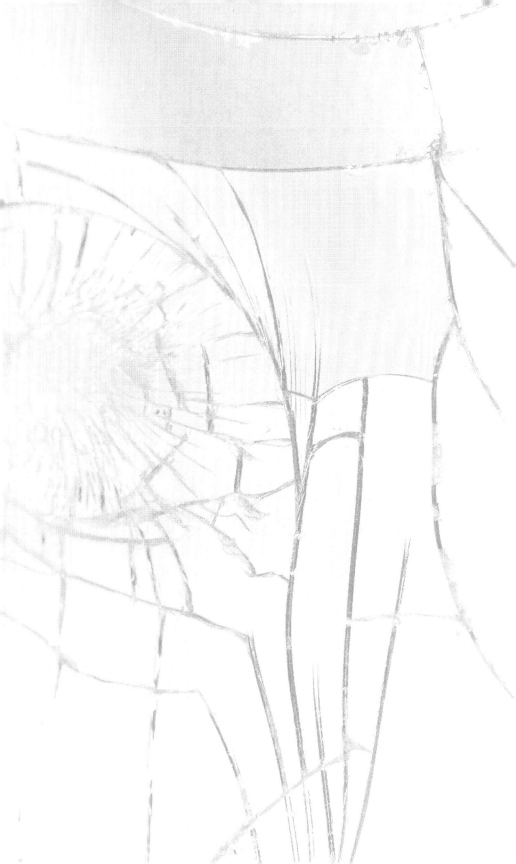

CHAPTER 8

What's Wrong with How I'm Thinking? Perceptual and Processing Issues

Focus on Self

The cardinal trademark of narcissism is the pathological focus on yourself, as opposed to being aware and attuned to the feelings, needs, and realities of those around you. People who struggle with narcissism have great difficulty in processing their experiences beyond their own frame of reference. The ability to step out of your own way of looking at things and to consider others' perspective is a crucial element in any relationship. This is the Achilles heel of those with narcissistic personalities that can impair their ability to attain and sustain healthy relationships.

This self-focus manifests in both the perceptual and processing aspects of interactions with other people. Perception refers to how we perceive or look at a particular experience, in terms of what we think is actually happening or how someone is treating us. People who are narcissistic typically perceive situations in terms of how they are affected by them and how it relates to their own needs, fears, or wants. They view the situation through the prism of their own unique experiences or baggage, which usually results in perceptions that are idiosyncratic, and do not conform to objective reality.

It is not at all uncommon for people who engage with narcissists to feel that they've distorted events or interactions in their lives in order to meet their need to protect their fragile egos. People become enormously frustrated with the inability of narcissists' to see something any other way than the way that they are seeing it. They resist an alternative viewpoint often while insisting that the other person "just doesn't get it," even though they are the ones who actually aren't getting it.

Processing refers to how you interpret an experience, and what thought patterns develop as a result of your perceptions. Narcissistic people often see themselves as the victim in situations, despite the fact that they are the ones doing the victimizing. As mentioned in Chapter 7, narcissists often utilize defense mechanisms to defend themselves against facing uncomfortable truths about themselves or to put the blame on the other person, even though, objectively speaking, they are the real problem.

They often develop narratives in their heads that reflect the baggage they experienced in their lives that may have damaged them in the first place, rather than reflecting what is actually, in reality, taking place. The inability to process one's experiences from a perspective of objective reality causes significant damage to relationships. This is so because sharing common experiences—and the bonding that ensues as a result—creates the foundation of a relationship. This is particularly true of the relationships that are essential to healthy living and life satisfaction: a marriage, a parent-child relationship, or a work partnership.

CASE EXAMPLE 19: HUMBERTO

Humberto was a 65-year-old, divorced entrepreneur, who came in for therapy with his much younger fiancée, Lily. They were having great difficulty in coming to terms on a prenuptial agreement that he was requiring her to sign. He needed her to agree to his terms to move forward with wedding plans, as she deeply wanted—especially since they had already been engaged for more than a year. Besides being controlling in general, Humberto was exceedingly so with regards to money, especially since his previous wife ended up with a large settlement after their expensive, difficult divorce. He was determined to make sure this wouldn't happen again, and he was absolutely unwilling to discuss wedding dates or venues until Lily signed the agreement.

For her part, Lily understood Humberto's negative experiences, and was trying to be earnest and fair in negotiating the agreement. However, the terms were so unfair and harsh, and, in her opinion, punitive, that she couldn't just sign the agreement as was, especially since her sister, an attorney, told her that it was one of the most unbalanced and outrageous prenuptial agreements she had ever seen. This was causing her much anxiety and angst, which Humberto saw as manipulative drama aimed at getting him to make concessions he didn't feel he should have to accept.

Humberto made the situation worse for Lily by turning it around in his head to make it look like he was the victim of excessive "demands" from her which were being "shoved down his throat." He perceived her as focusing only on his money, and being selfish and self-protective at his expense, even though she was actually quite other-centered and generous by nature. He felt he was being forced to compromise his financial future, despite the fact that he was a multimillionaire and she had limited resources as a restaurant hostess, and the fact—most importantly—that he was the one demanding to impose the prenup on her, and not the other way around. He could never see that he was the one putting her in the compromised position of signing an agreement that would leave her financially unstable, without a suitable home to live in, and forced to raise future children without adequate resources. Lily eventually broke off the engagement, prompting Humberto to convince himself, and anyone who agreed to listen to his rants about her, that this showed she only wanted his money after all.

Immaturity: Impulsive, Reactive, and Emotional Thinking

Conscious, deliberate, rational thought requires people to keep their emotions at bay and to allow only the "thinking" part of their brain to work through—or process—events. The brain is divided into two hemispheres, the right and the left. Logical, reality-based thinking takes place and is processed in the left hemisphere, unless the right brain—the home of emotions and "baggage" from the past—kicks in and hijacks the brain's processing mechanism.

Narcissistic people are much more likely to have experienced trauma that damaged their personalities. Traumatic memories are usually stored in the hippocampus, the memory center of the brain, and activated by the brain's emotional center, the limbic system. So, when an emotional event of some kind triggers a narcissist, he or she usually can't process the experience clearly and dispassionately. This happens because the intensity of the limbic system's reaction effectively shuts down the left brain's processing mechanism, leaving the individual too angry or enraged to think things through in a rational, calm, or effective manner. This is commonly referred to as an "amygdala hijack," in reference to the center of the limbic system, which gets intensely activated when one is highly triggered.

Susceptibility to amygdala hijacks is why narcissists typically have anger management problems. They most often have a disproportional amount of anger from their emotional baggage, usually based on some history of abuse. When triggered, the intensity of the limbic system's reaction shuts down the left brain's ability to process the experience which normally can help the individual work through it, and let it go or leave it behind. Instead, rage overcomes the person who is incapable of controlling his or her anger and usually lashes out with a vengeance that reflects the baggage inside more than the situation at hand.

In his seminal work on the neurobiology of trauma, *The Body Keeps the Score*, Dr. Bessel van der Kolk, undoubtedly the world's leading expert in the field, discusses how the nervous system encodes and absorbs trauma, which remains in the brain, raw, unprocessed, and ready to be reactivated when the person is triggered by stimuli that the brain associates with the original trauma. When a person experiences something reminiscent of earlier abuse or mistreatment, the brain unleashes the emotions connected to those stored memories. The person then reacts with the full force of the current trigger, as well as with the underlying emotional baggage that has been stored in the hippocampus.

This type of emotional reactivity and difficulty with managing anger feeds into a vicious cycle of damaged self-esteem, defensiveness against feeling badly about one's behavior, and damaged relationships that make the person feel even worse about themselves. So, when triggered, a narcissistic person, who already feels badly about himself, reacts in a way that negatively affects the people in his life. He then misprocesses the experience by blaming them for triggering him, which only alienates them even further. He then feels even worse when these people begin to act cold and aloof, because they feel that he mistreated or abused them. So, around and around the story goes.

Under-Incorporative Thinking

Years ago, in an attempt to make the old Rorschach test more objective and valid, the researcher John Exner devised a scoring system that allows psychodiagnosticians (psychologists who do psychological testing) to derive results that are more comprehensive and that describe a broader picture of how the individual who is being tested functions in various areas of his or her psychological life. One of the concepts that he developed was cognitive style, which emphasizes the processing system's incorporation of information from one's experiences.

Incorporative people take in an appropriate amount of information, and process their experiences in a way that allows for adequate under-standing and insight without thinking too much about it or not thinking it through enough. On the other hand, over-incorporative people tend to overanalyze or overthink things when triggered, and to act in an obsessive or perseverative way. They can't stop thinking about what happened, and they keep looping around their own cognitions in a seemingly purposeless way. They lack the ability to settle things in their mind or to come to some sort of satisfactory resolution.

At the opposite end of the spectrum lies people who are under-incor-porative in the way they react to their experiences. Under-incorporative people are impulsive; they react before considering all the factors they need to think about before taking some sort of action. They tend to react out of emotion, rather than responding based on deliberately thinking things through and deciding on an appropriate course of action. They can't stop to think, and take in all aspects of the situation, seeing things from different sides, and processing through the situation in a way that incorporates all its various aspects.

As a result, they often misfire, and react in a way that doesn't reflect the whole picture, but only the aspect that they see from their own frame of reference. Even with that, an under-incorporative person often can't see the entire picture based on his own perspective because of his impulsivity and reactivity. Failing to take in all aspects of a situation before responding impairs an individual's ability to use good judgment and to respond in ways that reflect all that occurred. Rather, his under-incorporative style forces him to react in ways that others see as impulsive, irrational, and immature.

Because of the way that trauma affects the brain, narcissistic individuals—who often experience trauma in their childhood, the period when personality is being formed—often react to stress or conflict in primitive, regressed ways. These responses fail to account for all the aspects of a situation, causing overreactions that are immature and not based in objective reality. Indeed, my experience has been that narcissistic people have a greater tendency to be under-incorporative in their cognitive style. Thus, they require therapy that can help teach them to slow down and take in all the information about a particular situation that they need to get a clear and comprehensive view. Then, based on the larger picture, they can make better, more conscious choices of how to respond in a way that will be more appropriate and effective in resolving things to the everyone's satisfaction, thus preserving relationships, rather than destroying them.

Irrational Thinking

Oftentimes, people with narcissistic personalities demonstrate completely irrational thinking that does not coincide with the reality that the people in their lives objectively experience. In the example above, Humberto had irrationally turned the situation around in his head in such a way that he became the victim, rather than seeing that he was forcing a very unpleasant process on his fiancée, and then imposed a solution on her that was, by all measures, unfair and unreasonable. Yet, he could not see the situation for what it was, and his irrational thinking prevented him from handling it in a manner that would have preserved the relationship.

This example shows a level of irrationality that is a distortion of reality, but to a degree still within some degree of sanity. However, in some extreme cases, especially when there is also some degree of co-morbid disorders, as in the case of a major mental illness such as Paranoid Disorder or Borderline Personality Disorder (see Chapter 6), the distortions can be almost of psychotic proportions.

CASE EXAMPLE 20: JAMES

James was an incest survivor, a victim of child sexual abuse involving his father. He was admittedly very self-centered, demanding, and harshly judgmental when people in his life failed to meet his needs or his unreasonably high standards of behavior. He clearly fulfilled the diagnostic requirements for Narcissistic Personality Disorder. However, he also had strong Borderline Personality Disorder traits and, from time to time, especially when stressed, would get paranoid and be totally out of reality. He was compulsively obsessed with being on time, and expected me to be on time, to the minute, for our sessions. This was nearly impossible for me to comply with, given the complexities of patients who often need a little more time, combined with my decidedly non-compulsive personality.

One day, he texted me that he was running late because of an intense thunderstorm that hit while he was driving, and that he was very stressed about it. He also asked if I was on time, because I tend to run late, so he had hoped that we would be in synch time-wise. I responded that I happened to be on time, because my previous patient had to leave early, but not to worry about it and to take his time and drive safely. He immediately called me, and became enraged that I deliberately made sure I would be on time in order to shame him. He accused me of telling him to take his time in order to cut down the time that I would have to spend with him. When I attempted to help him see that I was just trying to soothe his stress and to reassure him that it was OK to be a little late, he accused me of trying to cover up my outrageous behavior, and said he was entitled to extra time to compensate for it.

Only after he was able to calm down and get into his left brain, could James see things more objectively and realize that he was really interpreting my attempts to help him through the lens of abandonment. In his mind, all he could see were efforts to shame him and prepare for my eventual termination, because he knew "deep down" that I did not want to keep having to deal with the likes of him.

James's level of distortion is quasi-psychotic, and reflects the transient paranoid thinking often seen in Borderline Personality Disorder. Individuals who are simply narcissistic rarely display that level of distortion. However, the narcissistic personality within him also had to project blame onto me to deflect the shame that he felt for being late, especially since he held me to such a rigid standard of punctuality. These types of defensive distortions are common among people who have such damage to their personalities that they can't bear to face their flaws and failings, and instead, project the blame onto others.

Defensive Cognitive Distortions

As previously discussed in Chapter 7, defense mechanisms are used to deflect away responsibility for the problems that narcissists cause because of their behaviors that alienate people around them. Instead of facing the fact that it is they who are the problem in their relationships, they must distort reality and make it about the rest of the world who is really at fault for all of their shortcomings. These distortions are examples of perceptual and processing deficits that plague most narcissists, and create havoc in their relationships. Since they really do see reality the way that the distortions lead them to perceive or interpret them, they often actually believe that what they see or how they think are true representations of reality. Humberto really believed that Lily was trying to exploit him financially, although she was actually quite sincere in her desire to be respectful of his personal finances, and to be fiscally conservative. He sincerely felt that he was the victim here, and that he felt that he was deserving of empathy because of all that she was trying to do to take advantage of his superior financial status.

These defensive cognitive distortions are often difficult, if not impossible to correct because of the fragility of the ego that entrenches the distortion. It was impossible for Larry to really see what he was doing, because to do so, he had to face the fact that he was really bullying someone that he was supposed to love, honor, cherish, take care of, and keep safe. In his mind, "I'll take care of you fine as long as we are married. If we divorce, I don't give a damn what happens to you. You're on your own." It's not only the degree of selfishness that is the problem here. It is also, and perhaps more importantly, the total lack of awareness of how pernicious this behavior is in impacting the people that we are supposed to love, and to expect that they will want to stay in a relationship with us, despite how badly we treat them. That may be the most distorted of perceptions, which often lead to narcissistic spouses being shocked when their wife or husband finally asks for a divorce, or just leaves the house for good. Many narcissistic patients of mine, over the years, have reported to me that "they never saw it coming," when their spouse ends the marriage, or when their child leaves home and cuts off all communication, or stops allowing them to see their grandchildren. This total cluelessness, and lack of awareness of the severity of the impact of their damaging behavior, is often the most dramatic example of defensive distortion that causes them to implode all of their relationships.

CASE EXAMPLE 21: CARLOS

Carlos came in for treatment with his wife, Sarita, who was asking for a divorce after years of emotional abuse and lack of intimacy in their lives and after the last straw had occurred: she had contracted herpes, obviously from him, because she had never been with another man other than Carlos. He was shocked that she would react that way, because, in their Latin culture, infidelity was acceptable, and in his eyes, almost normative. He had also developed the habit of frequenting prostitutes and strip clubs, and even acted out at times with men.

"What's the big deal? Besides, she is never available to me anyway, because she's always too angry to want to be with me." Weeks later, when he discovered that she went out for coffee with a male co-worker, he flew into a rage, and shouted to her that she was a whore, and that he wanted her to leave her job. He never came to the realization that he was being outrageously hypocritical, and that he was projecting his own shame and indecency onto her, which ultimately resulted in her leaving the marriage. He used her leaving to play out the victim role, and to this day, is still convinced that he was basically a "good guy," whose wife decided to dump him, selfishly destroying the family in the process, in order to pursue her own self-serving interests.

CHAPTER 9

But You Don't Understand How I FEEL! Painful Emotions Associated with Narcissism

Because narcissism is often due to negative childhood experiences that damaged the child's sense of self and safety in the world, negative emotions are an invariable consequence that are usually quite intense. A range of unpleasant, uncomfortable emotions are common, including anger, rage, hurt, resentment, self-pitying, and hypercriticism, experienced either as discrete emotions or, often, jumbled together in a complex of negative emotions. This impedes the individual from experiencing any real degree of happiness or level of satisfaction.

Anger/Rage

Anger is an omnipresent emotion in the life of people who are dealing with narcissism. They frequently have anger management issues, resulting from an aggregate of baggage from old wounds accumulated over a lifetime of mistreatment, abuse, and neglect. Alternatively, they experienced overindulgence and entitlement from parents who failed to provide adequate discipline, thus stripping them of their ability to feel competent, autonomous, and empowered. The underlying dynamic is also often one of projection. People who are narcissistic have badly damaged egos and carry huge inner repositories of shame, blame, and self-hate that they cannot bear to face. So, in order to deflect these painful feelings, they blame others, and pour out their anger when they feel slighted or ignored. They do this to protect their delicate egos from dealing with the reality that they aren't as important as they would like to believe, or that they really aren't entitled to all of the attention and fame that believe they deserve.

People who developed narcissism from years of early abuse carry a "reservoir of rage," the results of years of accumulated mistreatment, disappointment, and hurt. It just sits inside the person's unconscious, a veritable time bomb that is ready to explode at the smallest of provocations. Anger is the emotional baseline for many narcissists. Being angry becomes a place of familiarity and comfort, the "go-to" place when something triggers their emotions. Over time, strong neural pathways—neurological connections that develop over time as a result of patterns of behaviors—that relate to anger and rage translate into habit patterns of rageful behavior that become the cornerstone of the individual personality. They just become angry people who live their lives looking for ways that others are showing disrespect, treating them badly, or ignoring them.

To make matters worse, because of the person's history of emotional upheaval, the usual coping skills, conflict resolution strategies, ability to delay reinforcement, and other more mature developmental steps that people usually achieve over time, fail to develop. The underdeveloped, immature narcissistic brain cannot deal with interpersonal stressors and triggers in ways that lead to successful conflict resolution. It is incapable of handling delicate situations in a mature way. Thus, narcissists overreact, become defensive, or simply explode, and generally sabotage any chances of salvaging relationships in their lives.

Worse yet, they use the defensive distortions discussed in Chapter 8 to turn the situations around and to create the illusion of victimhood; that serves only to reinforce and further build up their reservoir of rage. Most people cannot climb out of this vicious cycle unless they're able to tolerate an intensive therapeutic treatment program. The right therapy can help them unravel the convolution of underlying dynamics that has contributed to their misery and failure. More of that discussion will be found in Section III.

Wounded/Hurt

People who are narcissistic are easily wounded by what people do or say, and often find themselves hurt by what they experience. The neural pathway previously mentioned can help you understand part of this dynamic. Given the pervasive amount of mistreatment or abuse that narcissists often experience, they become programmed to expect to be wounded, and to experience hurt in their relationships. They come to view events through that prism.

Over the years, I have seen many patients who go through their lives ricocheting from one hurtful episode to the other, rarely able to recover from the previous one before the next one hits. Their lives are Shakespearean tragedies, filled with stories of pain, betrayal, and unrequited love, with them as the central figure, enduring endless years of profound disappointment. In addition, because of their exquisitely fragile egos, they are more easily wounded and offended than the norm, and they find themselves far less resilient to their perceived wounds.

People often avoid those who are too easily wounded or angered. No one likes the feeling of "walking on eggshells." But, no matter what anyone else does, people with narcissism often perceive other people's behavior as malevolent or hurtful. Therefore, family, friends and colleagues often prefer to just stay away, and avoid the frustration of always being the villain.

Parents who play the role of the often-mistreated wounded souls being betrayed by their selfish, uncaring children alienate those children to the point that they eventually become self-protective, less caring, and more separate. They must insulate themselves from the constant accusations and complaints of how hurt their parents are by the latest perceived insult or neglect. This only reinforces the narcissistic parent's self-perception as a perpetually wounded martyr, perpetuating the vicious cycle of woundedness and avoidance that usually spirals out of control until the relationship completely breaks down. It also becomes a self-fulfilling prophesy that ends up being exactly as the "wounded" individual expected in the first place.

Hypersensitive/Defensive

The hypersensitivity of narcissists frequently manifests by being "thin-skinned" and too easily hurt by behaviors that most people would consider benign or harmless. Hypersensitive people are like fields littered with active land mines for their children, spouses, friends, or parents. You never know what will hurt or offend them, because such a vast repository of potential triggers can cause them to feel wounded. Hypersensitivity can be the result of trauma, but it can also be a character trait, genetically programmed and inherited from generations of similarly disposed ancestors.

The personality of "The Highly Sensitive Child" can, but does not always, evolve into narcissism later in life, as the child—now an adult—comes to expect everyone to dance around his or her sensitivities. Such narcissists expect everyone to accommodate their extensive and often-changeable needs so they can feel safe and secure. Highly sensitive children often develop into adults who are emotionally high-maintenance, and require a tremendous amount of carefulness and attentiveness from other people to maintain their very labile emotional equilibrium. Others often see these adults as draining, bottomless pits of need and sensitivity, inevitably leading to one person after another transitioning out of their lives.

Self-Pitying/Self-Victimization

The concepts of self-pity and victimhood are closely connected with hypersensitivity and people who are easily hurt and wounded. Narcissists are often "career victims," positioning themselves as perennially hurt or victimized whenever they are involved in any interpersonal conflict. Nothing is ever their fault. The other guy is always wrong. They are always the victim. The other guy is always the villain. Period. The script never changes.

Narcissists spend much time in their lives feeling sorry for themselves, believing that they were short-changed and that their failings were due to some external force that prevented them from succeeding. They do not take responsibility for the actions that contributed to their failures in the first place. Self-pity also draws much-needed attention from other people, which works at times, often rather effectively. However, this pay-off usually lasts for only a short period before the other person comes to the realization that this persona of victimhood wears thin very quickly.

Victimhood also perpetuates the illusion that life's disappointments and hurts are a result of a magical curse that somehow descended down to blight the victim's life, thus leaving him or her "destined for failure." The victim is resigned to a life filled with hurt and disappointment for no specific reason, "just because..." This happens, not because they didn't work hard enough, or they expected things to be given to them on a silver platter, or because they had a significant role in whatever kept them from succeeding. It's "just because." People with narcissistic personalities often think very simplistically. They do not process things through, because that would require a higher level of awareness and honesty than they possess. They simply do not have the ego strength or the capacity to be introspective and emotionally honest enough to take responsibility for their shortcomings and misdeeds. Instead, they project blame onto others, shift the responsibility onto people around them, and play the victim role all too well.

Arrogant/Critical

Another dynamic often associated with narcissism is arrogance, the feeling of being superior, special, or above others in ability, standing, or status. As part of the need to deflect underlying feelings of defectiveness or inferiority, narcissistic people often, if not usually, create an artificially inflated sense of self. This reflects a feeling that they are superior to others in a variety of ways, which serves to protect their fragile egos from facing their very real deficiencies. This feeling of superiority often manifests itself through haughtiness, intolerance, and criticism of others, as the individual attempts to demonstrate the relative inferiority of those around him to buttress his underlying diminished sense of self.

What is interesting, if not ironic, is that even though narcissistic people are often arrogant in a way that demonstrates a marked insensitivity to the feelings of others, they are usually extremely sensitive about their own feelings, needs, and insecurities. In fact, hypersensitivity, and heightened reactivity to one's environment is often a hallmark of narcissism, and a common factor that contributes to the relationship difficulties usually associated with this type of personality.

Case Example 22: Margot

Margot was an attractive, 30-something professional, who grew up in a wealthy, overprotective family. Her mother, Elise, was, on the one hand, demanding, critical, and unaware of the intrusiveness of her behavior. On the other hand, her mother was also overindulgent and overly focused on Margot's physical appearance. She went to great lengths to accentuate her daughter's natural beauty with expensive clothes, makeovers, and cosmetic surgeries.

Margot was once married to a successful attorney, Tony, who divorced her several years ago. According to Margot, Tony was insensitive to her feelings and didn't understand her needs. He didn't realize that things affected her in a "special" way. She explained that most, if not all, of the people in her life had failed her, and were unwilling or unable to do what was needed to make her feel cared for and loved.

Elise reported that Margot was "always" a difficult, demanding child, and she admitted to having spoiled her when she was younger. According to Elise, Margot was frequently angry about what people had done to hurt or betray her. She got mad when people would invariably disappoint her in failing to come through on any of her multiple demands or expectations. She complained constantly about how she was the victim of the mistakes or deliberate mistreatment of the people around her. However, she failed to cite one instance in which she was at fault, or for that matter, had any responsibility in her frequent conflicts with others.

Margot came in for her appointment with an obvious resentment toward her mother for having pushed her to come for therapy. She focused on all of the evils and crimes that her mother had committed toward her over the years. She, then proceeded to discuss how her ex-husband had victimized her by leaving her, and to say that she was getting tired of all of the people in her life disappointing her and letting her down. The session was an endless stream of complaints about her life. When I asked how she may have contributed to any of these problems, she looked at me and said, "You just don't get it! This is not about ME! I am fine the way I am. It's about my life and all of the clowns in my world who have made me so miserable. They're the problem!"

This was the only time that I would see Margot. She failed to show up for her next appointment, and when I called her, she abruptly said that she would not come back for a follow up and that she was in the process of looking for a therapist who could understand her needs more adequately, because, "you obviously don't have a clue."

Margot was in intense pain, but it was she who actually did not have a clue: She didn't realize that she was the source of her own pain. Her narcissistic attitude and behavior had affected the people in her life in a way that caused them to be alienated and withdraw from her. The narcissistic defense mechanism distorted the situation in her mind to such an extent that she was convinced that they were the problem, and not her.

CHAPTER 10

Why Can't I Just Get Along? Impact of Narcissism on Relationships

Absence of Mutuality/Balance

Whether in the context of a marriage, a family, a work setting, or a friendship—the concept of mutuality, or the presence of balance in a relationship, is a fundamental ingredient for success. It is crucial in terms of needs being met and the ability to listen and to be responsive to the other person. Relationships with mutuality tend to last and grow, whereas those that are imbalanced and skewed to the needs of one person, tend to dissipate over time and eventually terminate. People tend to get fed up when they are the only ones who are listening, responding, or focusing on the needs of the other, and they usually end up transitioning out of the relationship, if at all possible. People don't want to be in, or stay in, a one-sided relationship, unless they have no choice. They may also be programmed to do so through their own childhood experiences and, therefore, just can't walk away.

People with narcissistic personalities often end up in one-sided relationships because of their endless needs and focus on themselves, and their inability to focus on or respond to others. When they talk to friends or relatives, they invariable turn the conversation toward themselves, and they rarely show any interest in the other person's life or feelings. This leaves those who try to communicate with them feeling empty, unimportant, and frustrated. What they are trying to talk about never gets addressed because of narcissists' need to make it about themselves. This usually alienates the other person, who finds that the conversation is an exercise in futility, especially in terms of being able to get any of their needs met or even in feeling that they matter at all. People with any amount of core or sense of self will eventually end this type of relationship. The only people who can tolerate such lack of mutuality are those who don't have much of a core or any sense that they also matter as a person, and those who grew up in narcissistic families in which this dynamic is all too familiar.

Communication Difficulties

Most people would agree that communication is the foundation of any relationship. The quality or effectiveness of communication often determines the relationship's satisfaction and viability, and the extent to which the partners wish to invest in it and in each other. Without good communication, relationships generally don't last. When communication is good, however, relationships tend to flourish, grow, and develop over time.

So, what constitutes good communication? The ability to listen is the most important factor in good communication. Good listening on the part of both partners allows both to feel heard and, hopefully, understood, which deepens their mutual connection. A relationship needs connectedness to flourish and develop. Without good, active listening, in which both parties feel genuinely heard, connection is impossible. Thus, good listening is a vital component of any relationship.

Unfortunately, narcissists are often poor listeners. To be a good listener, you need the ability to step out of yourself and your own frame of mind, in order to fully hear and comprehend what the other person is really saying. It is difficult for people who are narcissistic to listen effectively, because to do so, they must let go of themselves—what they are feeling, what they need, what's inside of their heads—and pay full attention to what the other person is saying.

Validation is another important component of effective communication. It requires letting people know that what they are saying is valid, that it is important, and that it makes sense. *It does not necessarily mean that you agree with them.* Rather, validation confirms that you feel that what they are saying needs to be considered carefully. It communicates respect, and helps the other person feel valued and heard, both of which contribute to a successful relationship.

Unfortunately, people with narcissistic personalities tend to be argumentative, and they need to be right in any disagreement or conflict of opinions. They often, if not always, are unable to validate other people's feelings or needs. Instead, they continue to argue the point or to express their feelings and needs relentlessly. Their fragile egos and stubborn need to be right interfere with their ability to validate another person. The tone and tenor of an argument could be soothed instantly if the narcissist could actively choose to find something, anything, to focus on and validate. That would create a greater possibility of a successful resolution to the argument. The skill of validation is a fundamental component of conflict resolution, which is addressed in more depth in Chapter 17.

You can use several effective communication strategies to build safety and connection in relationships. The first, "I statements," remove the confrontational, accusatory use of "you" that can often bring out defensiveness in other people. For example, instead of saying, "You were really cruel to me when you said…," you say, "I am uncomfortable and hurt by what was said to me earlier." With the focus on how something affected you, instead of what you think of the person for saying it, you compel people to deal with you and your feelings, instead of defending themselves or their behavior.

Similarly, when you describe your feelings, instead of their behavior, you make it difficult for them to deflect away from how they acted. It more likely forces them to deal with your feelings. The claim that someone is cruel is a matter of debate; the person with narcissism can easily dispute or dismiss it. But your feelings of discomfort or hurt cannot be easily argued about or ignored.

Finally, using a passive voice statement ("Mistakes were made") instead of an active voice one ("You made a mistake") is also less likely to elicit defensive reactions. For example, instead of saying, "You are really a mess; you screwed up my day by being so late," which can be interpreted as a direct attack or accusation, you can say, "My day was messed up because I was made to be late. I am really frustrated." This response includes an "I" statement and a feeling statement. It is phrased in passive voice, which softens it considerably, making it more possible for the other person to respond in a conciliatory manner. This approach is more effective in preserving and building a relationship than one that is confrontational and directed against the individual.

Entitlement

People with narcissistic personalities often feel entitled in relationships. That can cause other people to feel exploited, pressured, or victimized. Entitlement means feeling that you are special and deserve special treatment, or that things are coming to you, just because of who you are. For example, adult children who feel that they deserve to be supported by their parents because Mom and Dad are wealthy, or because they believe the folks didn't treat them fairly compared to their siblings, embody entitlement.

Entitlement is toxic to relationships, because it causes resentment. It adds to the pressure on people who feel exploited and abused by the demands placed upon them in their relationships with narcissistic, entitled individuals. Oftentimes, these individuals are not even aware that their sense of entitlement is inappropriate or destructive to their relationships. They are so focused on their needs, and their perception that they have things "coming to them," that they are completely unaware of their destructive impact on other people. Entitlement is like the oxygen they breathe—an inextricable part of the way they perceive themselves in relationship to the world. It is crucial to step back, and to assess when you may be truly entitled to something versus not being entitled at all, which is more likely.

Fighting the curse of entitlement goes back to humility. People who feel entitled to having things that are not rightfully theirs, or who feel that they deserve special treatment or recognition, are basically arrogant. They maintain that the world is there to meet their needs, and that they should be able to have whatever they want. The best antidote to that pernicious way of thinking is to be humble, to realize that we have to earn most of what we want in life, and that we, in fact, do not have it coming to us. Arrogant people who feel entitled are only reinforcing their underlying lack of self-esteem and insecurity, because they deprive themselves of the emotional benefits of hard work. They would feel better if they honestly earned what they want, instead of just receiving it because they are entitled or indulged. Conversely, when you work hard and meet your goals, you build up a positive self-image as an industrious, self-reliant person who has earned what he has. This, in turn, reinforces hard work and, thus, makes someone more likely to continue to be earnest and conscientious in earning what he receives.

Intimacy Issues

Because of underlying insecurities, lack of self-esteem, and feelings of deficiency and defectiveness, people with narcissistic personalities often avoid intimacy. This is often because, at an unconscious level, they fear exposing their dark underside to people around them. At a core level, they are ashamed and fearful of people knowing who they really are, so they push people away if they feel that they are getting too close. Narcissists are notorious for sabotaging relationships, and either not allowing true intimacy, or being fundamentally unable to be intimate. Being emotionally transparent is a key ingredient in a successful relationship, and people with narcissistic personalities often go through multiple relationships or marriages, because of their lack of ability to share real intimacy.

This does not mean that people with this type of personality cannot function sexually within a relationship. With people who are narcissistic, sexual behavior is not necessarily associated with intimacy. For them, sex is often centered on winning a conquest, deriving pleasure, boasting of the sexual encounter to others, or feeding a damaged ego. It involves everything but true intimacy. Intimacy requires sharing loving feelings, pleasuring your partner, revealing intimate details of your life to bring closeness to the relationship, and expressing vulnerability that brings a sense of openness and safety to the partnership.

Achieving intimacy involves becoming more comfortable with who you are as a person, and feeling safe enough to share what is inside of you with your partner. Intimacy is about being real and honest about your feelings, and allowing someone into your inner world. Feeling whole and content with who you are, with all of your flaws and shortcomings, is an essential step toward being more comfortable with being intimate. Working toward that goal in therapy can help you achieve it. Finally, intimacy requires healing the wounds that caused the narcissism in the first place, so that the person can be at peace internally and accept what is, instead of striving to be something or someone else.

Parenting Issues

Being a parent is perhaps the most selfless thing that we do. Bringing children into the world, nurturing and caring for them, and providing protection and financial support is a constant, and often never-ending, effort and sacrifice. Being an *effective* parent requires even more effort and ability, since it takes the capacity to put our children and their needs first, before our feelings, wants, frustrations, and other competing interests. Doing a good job as a parent is not for the faint of heart; it takes tremendous self-discipline, hard work, and infinite patience. Most importantly, though, it requires us to be primarily focused on our children's feelings and needs, and not our own.

This is essentially the challenge that people with narcissistic personalities have in raising healthy, confident children. When a child becomes cantankerous, demanding, or angry, as invariably happens in normal family life, parents who are effective in their child-rearing practices will assess the situation and determine the most appropriate way to handle it. They take the child's temperament, current situation, and unique needs into account, and then respond accordingly. They make decisions based on their child's needs, not how the child is affecting them. For the narcissistic parent, however, a temper tantrum becomes a personal attack that warrants a strong emotional or physical reaction. It is a direct affront to his or her role as a parent, and often triggers feelings of rage, contempt, or disdain. The focus is not on how to neutralize the child's despair effectively, but rather on how to defend the parent's compromised position as an authority figure. Narcissistic parents perceive that a child who should know his or her place and should be compliant and obedient at all times is attacking them. The reality of a narcissistic parent offers little, if any, room for a child's self-expression or frustration—especially if it conflicts with the parent's agenda or threatens his or her very delicate ego.

CASE EXAMPLE 23: MACK

The youngest of five boys raised in a blue-collar family in rural Ohio, Mack was more affected by his alcoholic father's rage attacks than his brothers because he was the least obedient of the crew. His defiance invariably triggered his father, especially when he was drunk. Bright and fiercely independent, Mack became a highly successful real estate developer and married his attractive sales representative, Elena, with whom he raised two sons, Jarrod and Marco. Mack was a controlling, dominating figure in the family, and he demanded absolute obedience from his wife and children. Any attempts at individual expression or choice would usually end up with Mack flying into a fit of rage. Elena learned early on in the marriage that, in order to maintain peace in the family, she needed to defer to Mack and to avoid confrontation at all cost.

As they grew up, both boys reacted poorly to Mack's authoritarian style and rage attacks, as well as their mother's passivity, and became oppositional and argumentative. This only provoked their father even more, and the cycle of rage continued through their adolescence and young adult years. Mack's reaction to his sons reflected his narcissistic narrative that he was the victim of his children's disrespect and lack of appreciation for all that he did for his family, rather than the actual reality—that they were merely mirroring his own rage and acting out their feelings about his abusive behavior toward his family.

When they graduated from college, they both distanced themselves from their father, and moved to another city, where they went into business together. Elena eventually got the help she needed to file for divorce, leaving Mack alone, always the victim, and completely unaware of the toxic effects of his anger and rage—still echoing his father's pattern.

Overcoming Anger

Working on becoming a more effective, other-centered parent takes work, but success is not impossible, even for those whose narcissistic personalities have previously impeded their ability to parent effectively. The steps to take in accomplishing this goal include:

1. Learning to put yourself into the mind and heart of your child, asking yourself basic questions such as, "What is my child feeling right now?" or "What does my child need from me right now?" This forces you out of the self-centered way of reacting to a child who is acting out, and points you toward a more other-centered approach that is far more likely to be more effective.

2. Be more aware of what you are feeling internally. Identify your feelings in a way that enables you to process them more adequately and, hopefully, diffuse them. Asking yourself questions such as, "What am I feeling now, and why am I feeling it?", or "How can I reframe these feelings so that I can be more in control emotionally, and be more effective in dealing with this?", can be enormously helpful in diffusing the inferno that is exploding inside of you.

3. If you feel that you are losing control of your emotions, take a break, remove yourself from the situation, and go to a quiet, calm room (bathrooms work great for this). Breathe deeply, with your eyes closed, and repeat a mantra such as "calm" or "relax" that can help you regain your composure, and enable you to go back and more effectively tackle steps one and two above.

These steps are, in effect, a way for a narcissistic people to push themselves out of the fire and fury of their right brain, where the emotional center of the brain resides. The amygdala is the central component of the limbic systems, which gets activated when someone is emotionally triggered. Rage, often called a "limbic hijack," is a common occurrence among people with narcissistic personalities, because they are easily triggered and quick to anger.

By removing themselves from the triggering situation, and by asking questions that force them to think about what is going on instead of reacting emotionally, they actually force themselves out of the activated right brain and into the calmer, more logical, left brain. This is the part of the nervous system that facilitates processing and helps people think their way out of rage. They can then assess what is happening more calmly and decide what options they have for better managing the situation without causing further damage to their children and their relationships with them, which are often difficult to repair.

This is the fundamental difference between reacting and responding. Reactions are involuntary emotional reflexes that happen without any active thought or processing. Reactions occur impulsively, without conscious regard for the consequences or damage that they will invariably cause. Responses, on the other hand, are conscious, deliberate attempts to deal effectively with situations, which are a result of the active processing of events that are being experienced, as well as the feelings that result from these events. The goal is to become thoughtful responders who consider their options for managing situations, and then implement them accordingly, and to stop reacting out of raw emotion in ways that alienate others, including their children.

Many people with narcissistic personalities were emotionally abused as children. This damaged their sense of self, and bred narcissism as a defense against assault. If that describes you, and you find that you are treating your children as you were treated, try to muster a higher level of awareness and remember that this kind of adult behavior damaged you in the first place. If you do not get the right support, you will cause similar damage to your own children, perpetuating the cycle of abuse and damage to the next generation.

Most people with narcissism are not inherently bad. In fact, most are basically well-meaning in their desire to be better parents than their parents were. However, without effective help and clear efforts to change the patterns of behavior that permeated the dynamics of their family of origin, people are largely destined to "repeat the sins of the fathers," and to recreate the abuse they endured as children. Fortunately, with the right assistance and coaching, and a strong, enduring effort to change, most people on the spectrum of narcissism can modify, if not eradicate, their destructive behavior patterns and work toward being the loving parents they want to become.

Another model of narcissism warrants mention, in terms of how narcissistic parents struggle to nurture and raise children in a healthy, effective manner. Due to neglect or abuse, many parents with this type of personality did not get nurtured or built up by their parents. They tend to look to their children for the love, attention or validation that they did not receive as children. Although not necessarily angry or abusive, these parents are damaging in their own ways by being needy and demanding, and by relying on their children to meet their emotional needs—as well as to help them fulfill their parental responsibilities and duties. These children are often referred to as "parentified" children, since they end up parenting their parents, and focusing on their mother's or father's feelings and needs, instead of relying on their parents to meet their own emotional needs.

Effects of Narcissism on Children

There has been considerable research and literature on narcissistic parents, and their effects on children. Although there are many aspects to this dynamic, several key factors tend to emerge that may assist us in understanding how parents who are angry and self-centered, or needy and dependent, affect their children.

1. Children of narcissistic parents often experience their own forms of insecurity and lack of self-esteem. Lacking effective parenting that is necessary for healthy confidence and successful relationships, they often grow into insecure, anxious adults who end up in failed relationships due to an inability to attach in a healthy manner. Their anxiety and insecurities manifest in a variety of ways that impede their ability to function, and to flourish in their lives.

2. Children of narcissists also can grow up being angry and depressed as adults, because of the lack of love and nurturance that they required as children. They are endlessly resentful and pessimistic about relationships, since their early experiences were so hurtful and damaging. They tend to either sabotage relationships with their negativity and anger, or avoid them altogether.

3. Other children of narcissists model after their parents, and become narcissists themselves. They recreate the dynamic that they experience, and end up with a series of failed relationships due to abusive, controlling behaviors that drives their partners away. Their needs are always paramount, and they have no ability to understand, anticipate, or meet the needs of their partners, who eventually grow tired of the lack of reciprocity, and end up terminating the relationship.

4. Others become "anti-narcissistic," as was discussed earlier, which describes individuals who are highly sensitive to the feelings and needs of others, have difficulty identifying or expressing their own needs, and have a high tolerance for narcissistic behavior. This heightened sensitivity to others developed as a result of a conditioned need to be highly attuned to their parents, lest they trigger their criticism or rage. They often end up attracting narcissists, and thus recreating the same type of marriage that they experienced as children. They are attracted to what is familiar, and often attract these type of partners, because they are perceived by them as being people who can be easily controlled and manipulated into fulfilling their every need.

Regardless of the manner in which people who grew up with narcissistic parents are affected by their early experiences, it is uncommon that children are left unscathed by their parents' narcissistic behaviors. Although there are relatively rare instances of highly resilient people who grew up in narcissistic homes, and have healthy, successful relationships, the vast majority of children of narcissistic parents are adversely affected by their upbringings, and end up being generally unhappy, with difficulty managing relationships in most, if not all, aspects of their lives.

CHAPTER 11

I Just Want to Make It BIG: Narcissism and Excessive Need for Achievement

---

CASE EXAMPLE 24: SARA

Sara was an only child of Holocaust survivors. They both lost their parents when they were young and suffered unspeakable horrors during the war years. They met after the war in a Displaced Persons camp in Germany, and married mostly out of a sense of loneliness and a determination to rebuild their shattered lives, rather than any sense of love or compatibility. In fact, they were highly incompatible, both with strong, contentious personalities, each trying to control the other. When they had Sara after several years of infertility due to trauma that Sara's mother experienced in a concentration camp, they at first showered her with much attention and indulged her every whim. However, after she began to assert her independence as an emerging adolescent, they both became controlling and abusive, fearing that she might eventually abandon their lifestyle and leave their lives forever. However, the more controlling they were, the more rebellious and angry she became. In time, Sara left home before graduating from high school, seeking opportunities "out there" that she thought would lead to fame and fortune.

However, her journey was plagued by a series of failed relationships that were undermined by her angry tirades, demands for attention and material possessions, and the need to control her partners' every move. She was possessed with the dream of becoming a huge success in business, and began to amass a small fortune with risky business ventures that proved to be highly lucrative. She spent her money freely, and began to develop a shopping addiction, with a particular focus on accumulating a small arsenal of expensive designer clothes and handbags, many of which sat, unused, in her rather large walk-in closet.

As her business schemes turned sour, however, her finances began to crumble; yet her need to shop and to attract attention through her expenditures remained unabated. She eventually lost her home due to neglecting her businesses, and ended up going bankrupt and moving back home to live with her recently widowed mother. They fought constantly, and ended up coming in for help to manage their unmanageable relationship. Although her mother did try to work on herself and to find a way to deal with her very difficult daughter more effectively, Sara became quickly frustrated with the therapy process, because her real goal was to get her mother to buy her an apartment so that she could move out. Her mother did not want to be taken advantage of, and I encouraged her to stand her ground. She was right not to enable Sara's entitlement and abusive behaviors. In reaction, Sara abruptly terminated therapy, and they continued to make each other's lives miserable until Sara once again left the family home, never to be heard from again.

As we just read in the sad story of Sara, her excessive need for fame and fortune led to her personal and financial demise. While her emphasis on monetary success and material possessions brought her much-needed attention, it also eventually resulted in the tragic collapse of her formerly fashionable life. Narcissism often leads to unrealistic dreams of fantastic fame and wealth, which is the subject of this chapter.

Grandiosity

One of the cardinal trademarks of narcissism is grandiosity, or fantasies and dreams of wild success that leads to attention and fame. To compensate for the underlying inadequacies associated with narcissism, people with this disorder often put all of their energies toward building successful financial empires or being a star in the entertainment business, or becoming a powerful politician. Their ambitions, however, are often beyond their realistic abilities, so they end up miserable about their inability to achieve their unachievable, lofty goals. They spend their lives resenting the success of those who are undoubtedly less talented or brilliant than they are. Or, if they achieve the success they dreamed of, they usually are not satisfied with that level of achievement, and focus on even loftier goals or on resenting those who are even more wealthy or famous than they are.

Grandiosity originates in the artificially inflated egos narcissists develop to compensate for their lack of self-esteem and for the inadequacy buried deep beneath their bloated façade. These deeply deflated souls are desperate to prove their real worth by achieving huge measures of success so they can finally convince themselves that they are worthy of praise and admiration, something their real, deflated selves could never experience.

Sadly, grandiose people never really earn the real respect of those around them, although these people may act as if they admire them to avoid unpleasant encounters. In truth, they don't respect them. They may even secretly loathe them for their bombastic, self-aggrandizing behavior. Even though grandiose narcissists convince themselves that others love and admire them for their extraordinary achievements, at some level, they know the awful truth—that they are seen as arrogant fools who try to intimidate those around them or buy their loyalty and admiration. Meanwhile, their relatives and employees honestly can't stand them, and they feel saddled with having to feed their enormous egos with praise and false admiration. They know they can't take the risk of being honest about how they really feel.

Once again, we come back to the basic principle of humility as the preferred antidote to the challenge of narcissism and, in particular, grandiosity. Once people realize that basic humility—the ability to be humble and to respect the dignity of those around them—is the ticket to sincere respect and admiration, their lives can, indeed, turn around. With humility, they can achieve successful relationships and genuine life satisfaction.

Unrealistic Goals

As was discussed in Chapter 8, narcissistic people often deeply believe perceptual and cognitive distortions that lead to unrealistic feelings and expectations. This can also manifest in unreasonable, unrealistic goals stemming from the grandiose needs to be famous or wealthy. Quite often, people with narcissistic personalities fantasize about goals that are beyond their capacity. In the process, they waste valuable resources, time, and effort to achieve the unachievable. Every US presidential election cycle features at least a few noticeably unnoticed "candidates" who have absolutely no chance of being elected. They insist on running, and stay in the race well beyond the point when it becomes obvious that their run for the White House is painfully futile. Yet, they doggedly remain in the hunt, oblivious to the public perception that they are egotistical fools.

Others pursue modeling careers, although they are not particularly attractive. They convince themselves that they are one "break" away from a glamorous career in modeling. Still others invest in high profile, but high-risk business ventures that promise a quick fortune, and find themselves with nothing to show for their investment except embarrassment and disappointment. They share the common denominators of an unrealistic appraisal of their actual potential to achieve unrealistic goals and an excessive need for the admiration and attention they feel they deserve.

Work Ethic Problems

Most people find that a good work ethic is key to achieving their personal goals. Success doesn't usually come randomly. Usually, you need all of the elements of plain old hard work to achieve it.

So, what are the elements of a good work ethic? First, and perhaps foremost, is personal integrity. This involves honesty, sincerity, and the ability to keep your word. Without integrity, no real work ethic can emerge. The ability to be trusted and trustworthy, and to be always honest is the cornerstone of integrity. Second, the desire to work hard, be conscientious, and perform your required duties and responsibilities are also important elements of a good work ethic. Third, the ability to take orders from your superiors, maintain a good attitude while working, and exhibit positive behavior toward your co-workers are all important aspects of a good work ethic. Finally, those with a good work ethic are reliable and consistent in their job performance, regardless of challenges that may come up.

People who are narcissistic often have problems with their work ethic at several different levels. Because of issues of entitlement, grandiosity, and superiority, narcissists are notoriously poor workers. They find it very difficult to take orders or to follow through on tasks and responsibilities that require discipline, or that are not interesting or naturally exciting. They prefer having free time, if given a choice, and are often the last to come to work and the first to leave. They tend to have poor attitudes, since they too often feel that the job at hand is beneath them or designed for people with lesser abilities or experience. Lastly, narcissists tend to be unreliable and inconsistent, since they tend to do the things they want to do, when they want to do them, rather than doing what they must do at the designated time. They generally resist being controlled, and are usually better suited to being their own bosses, so they are free to be in the driver's seat, deciding what they will do, and in their own preferred time frame.

Delay of Gratification

Children have difficulty in delaying gratification. They're usually impulsive in terms of wanting what they want right now, instead of being able to wait until later. Like children, narcissists have great difficulty delaying gratification. This can cause problems in the workplace, as one often must wait until a specified time before "perks" become available, or before you accrue enough time for it to be converted into time off. People with narcissistic personalities, and related issues of entitlement and grandiosity, feel that they are entitled to such perks because of their talents or status, even though they haven't really earned them.

Being able to delay gratification is a mark of emotional maturity, which is often lacking in narcissists. But people can acquire this skill over time. They can learn to tolerate the frustration of delayed gratification through the use of therapeutic techniques designed to build up frustration tolerance. Cognitive methods which help reframe such delays can help someone develop the maturity to cope with frustration and to process things in a way that enables them to deal with situations in which they are unable to get what they want when they want it. Over time, people can manage the negative emotions that come up when they're frustrated and can become more patient or accepting of situations that are not to their liking. This can be enormously helpful in the workplace, as well as in personal relationships that require sacrifice or negotiation for the sake of peaceful cooperation.

High Achievers

Many high achievers become so because of narcissistic traits that cause them to be driven to succeed. The need for recognition of their special abilities and talents, as well as for material wealth, push many people to achieve beyond the level of their peers. This is not necessarily bad, as long as they maintain some balance and do not unduly compromise their family life. Unfortunately, many high achievers accomplish their goals at the expense of personal relationships and family life, and end up losing what you would think are far more important: their marriage, their families, and their relationships with their children. Their priorities are skewed in terms of how they define true success. For these high achievers, financial success or political power is the ultimate goal. That's how they define success, so their personal relationships become secondary. As a result, their relationships suffer and succumb to their preferred goals. That is one of the reasons why so many rich and powerful people go through multiple divorces; they don't know how to order their priorities properly.

This doesn't have to be the case with talented and driven people. You can achieve tremendous success, but stay grounded in terms of what is really important. Even people with narcissistic personalities can come to understand that their personal relationships are their true priorities, the enduring achievements of their lives. Other types of successes can be fleeting or impermanent. Many people have lost successful businesses or experienced political setbacks. However, if your relationships and family life are strong, they can last forever. That means making them your most important priority. Take Carlos, for example.

CASE EXAMPLE 25: CARLOS

Plagued with the feeling that he lived in the shadow of his hugely successful brother who started a major travel website, Carlos worked feverishly over long hours to build up his fledgling law practice. He frequently stayed in the office until after 11 p.m. His wife, Clarita, who was a de facto single parent, deeply resented his lack of involvement in the family, and his workaholic personality. She found that when she tried to get him to be more balanced with regard to his family life, Carlos would invariably become defensive and complain that she didn't appreciate his hard work and ambition to make things better for the family. Clarita felt trapped because she had no voice in their marriage and because he would make her feel guilty and regretful if she said anything at all.

Over time, she withdrew from him emotionally and sexually, and he complained bitterly that she was failing in her role as a wife. When she tried to explain that she had just shut down because he was never home and didn't participate in their family life as a husband or father, he lost it with her and said that she was ungrateful and spoiled. When they came into my office, they were on the verge of divorce, with both feeling very much misunderstood and taken for granted.

In time, Carlos was able to understand that his intense work habits were a futile attempt to compete with his brother and compensate for his underlying feelings of inadequacy. At last, he saw that he had misplaced his priorities by making work more important than his wife and family. Only then was the marriage able to recover. As he began to stick to a schedule and to get home early enough to engage with his family, Clarita became more loving and attentive to him. Over time they both realized that they did not want to lose each other, and they each worked hard to make the other more of a priority.

CHAPTER 12

Where Is G-d When You Need Him? Challenges to Spirituality

In working with narcissists for more than 30 years, I have noticed that many have difficulty maintaining the spiritual connection that they once had, or, as is often the case, never developed in the first place. To understand this often-seen phenomenon, let's first look at what we actually mean by spirituality, and then we will examine how narcissism affects one's ability to maintain, or attain, a spiritual connection.

Narcissism and Spirituality—Definitions

The American Heritage Dictionary defines something spiritual as "relating to, consisting of or having the nature of spirit, not tangible or material; of, concerned with or affecting the soul; of, from or pertaining to G-d…. sacred."

In more practical terms, spirituality can also be characterized as an ability to connect with an awareness that there is something, or some sort of force, that exists at a level higher than ourselves. In 12-step addiction terms, it is referred to as one's "higher power," an entity that is greater than ourselves, which we feel has an influence over our lives, usually defined by our cultural or religious upbringing. For many of us, G-d in various forms is that higher power, the Creator, the One we turn to for insight, guidance, and strength. For some of us, spirituality is a deep connection with the universe, or an energy or life force that enables us to think and feel at a greater depth, or to experience life with a higher degree of consciousness.

In short, spirituality offers a way of living that transcends our day-to-day experience, and transports us to a higher level of being.

Spirituality Blockers

Quite often, narcissists have difficulty connecting spiritually, because it requires an acknowledgement that there is something greater than you and that you're not omnipotent. It also requires an ability to be honest with yourself and to assess what you need to do to improve and become a better person.

This requires a degree of humility, an awareness that human beings, are, indeed, not G-d, and that as humans, we are actually quite imperfect, and in constant need of refinement and improvement. Spirituality enables us to look more deeply inside of ourselves, but narcissism often prevents us from doing so, because such introspection is too threatening for fragile egos. Insight and self-awareness are often very limited in people who are narcissistic, because defense mechanisms (as mentioned in Chapter 7) prevent them from seeing themselves objectively and honestly. However, such insight is the salient ingredient that allows spirituality and self-growth to take root, but attaining it is often difficult for people with narcissistic personalities.

Other factors associated with narcissism seem to block a person's spiritual potential, including arrogance and self-aggrandizement, as discussed in Chapter 9. These personality features leave no room for anything at a higher level than the self. This often leads narcissists to the delusional conclusion that they cannot gain anything by "giving themselves over to G-d," because they know everything they need to know, and no one, or anything, can teach them much.

Problems with Authority

Many people who are narcissistic have problems dealing with authority figures, usually because of the issue of control. People with these personality features are often quite resistant to the idea of being controlled, and as a result find it difficult to adhere to rules and limits. As mentioned in Chapter 6, co-morbid personality features such as Antisocial Personality involve an inability to defer to authority, respect societal norms, follow rules, or respect boundaries. Having a spiritual life involves a deep awareness of and a commitment to some form of a higher power or religious belief system that can provide a sense of order and structure to your life. This inherently involves an acceptance of the need to have an authority figure to whom you communicate through prayer, meditation, or other spiritual channel. Such practices help you develop and maintain a relationship with that figure, be it G-d, or any religious figure or concept that you have incorporated in your life. This also necessitates an ability to defer to that figure, or to subjugate yourself, in recognition that this higher power is indeed *higher* than yourself, and that you, therefore, are, by definition, lower than that higher power.

This concept of being lower than, or needing to defer to a higher power, is quite difficult for people with narcissistic personalities, because the very concept of being inferior to anyone, or anything, including G-d, threatens their fragile egos. Their self-concept requires being ahead of, better than, or top of their competitors, at all times. Being vulnerable, or weak, is difficult for them to tolerate. People with this kind of personality often can't defer to a stronger or more powerful entity. Developing this kind of spiritual relationship also requires a fair degree of humility and an awareness of personal imperfection. This often involves turning to G-d, or one's higher power, for help or spiritual strength to persevere when challenged. Narcissistic people lack the humility this requires. They tend to remain stubbornly self-reliant when challenged, refusing to turn to anyone or anything for assistance. Otherwise, they must face the reality that they are not as wonderful as they have led themselves to believe, or that they are more vulnerable and flawed than their defense mechanisms have allowed them to face.

Self-Sacrifice

Living a spiritual life often requires the ability to set aside selfish desires, or to sacrifice needs or wants for a higher spiritual purpose. This can take many forms, such as giving charity or tithing, which require allocating a portion of your earnings to help people who are less fortunate. It can also manifest in the way that we choose to eat, whether it is being a vegetarian, living a healthy lifestyle, following religious dietary laws, or adhering to other ethical or moral principles. Choosing not to indulge in certain foods because they violate intangible religious laws or ethical values requires a great deal of self-discipline, and the ability to say no to our impulses, something self-centered people often have difficulty maintaining consistently. Feelings of entitlement make it hard to develop a cognitive framework that allows for self-sacrifice. Narcissism keeps a person living only in the moment, without being aware of a higher purpose or in touch with a need for self-actualization.

Having a pattern of giving in to selfish impulses makes it difficult, if not impossible, to develop a sense of spirituality. Instead, the narcissistic personality focuses exclusively on what I want or what I need, as opposed to what is expected of me, or what I want to accomplish in this life, and the life beyond. The ability to sacrifice in the short run for long-term gain is a cornerstone of spirituality. That is why people with narcissistic personalities often find it difficult to live a meaningful spiritual life.

Spirituality also involves having goals directed toward self-improvement or actualization. Spiritual goals may include a wide array of endeavors, such as being more effective in your relationships, feeling more connected with a Higher Power, being more charitable or generous, or living a more disciplined life. These rather lofty goals are rarely on the radar of narcissistic people, who often have an entirely different vision of what they would like to accomplish.

Life Goals

People's goals often define them. Altruistic people aim to improve the lives of other people and to find ways to help people with no expectation of anything in return. Idealistic individuals strive to make the universe a better place and to look for ways to perfect a very imperfect world. Naturalists or environmentalists look to keep the Earth clean and safe, not only for themselves and their loved ones, but for future generations. The goal of family-oriented people is to provide for their families, and to give their children the foundation to live productive lives, and to raise productive children of their own.

The common denominator is that these individuals don't focus on themselves, or what they need or want. Rather, their life's goals involve making a difference for the common good. Their goals reflect this focus, and help them achieve a sense of spirituality on their own terms, and in ways that are deeply meaningful for them.

However, people with narcissistic personalities often set very limited goals based on self-serving aspirations. They focus on how to achieve fame and fortune, quite literally, and their goals reflect the need to be known and admired. Their sole focus may be accumulating the financial means to acquire what they need to feel successful and respected. They become intent on acquiring the material possessions that they have dreamed of or craved throughout their lives. Whether it is a larger house in a better location, the ultimate luxury car, that expensive watch that they saw someone famous wearing, diamond earrings, or the cosmetic surgery that will make them look more perfect, their goals are self-centered. They aim for something that will enhance their own lives, not the lives of other people. Lofty ideals typically are not on their radar screens. If they are charitable, getting attention or recognition may be their underlying purpose. Donors of large gifts often care most about how their names will be credited or displayed, as in endowment trusts or a building named after them or their family.

Volunteers may focus on how a charity will thank or recognize them, rather than on the impact that their work will have on the organization or its constituents. Fantasies of being honored or publicly recognized in a grand fashion preoccupy their minds, and become the purpose of their involvement, rather than the work at hand. Their goals are much more in the moment, or in the immediate future, and more directed toward themselves rather than the goal of fulfilling broader philanthropic ideals and causes.

Spiritual Connection as an Antidote to Narcissism

We can infer from this discussion that spirituality can play a major role, in becoming a less narcissistic, more other-centered person. Although it is true that working on becoming less narcissistic can help you to become more spiritual, the reverse may be true, as well. By working on your spirituality, you can also, at the same time, diminish the narcissism that is in your personality. Living a more genuine, spiritual life is almost antithetical to being narcissistic, and can help you to become less self-involved, and more attuned to the world around you.

However, making the transition to becoming more spiritual is challenging, especially if you are generally not very spiritually oriented. Years back, there was some talk of a "spiritual gene" that strongly influenced a person's propensity to experience spirituality. The debate about the existence of such a gene rages on, but we do know that some people are more inclined to experience or seek spirituality than others. Although the genetic heritability of such spiritual potential is quite tentative, clearly individual spiritual experiences are complex, in that other factors beyond genetics influence the attainment of spirituality.

Choosing to read books or articles that broaden your perspective on spiritual thinking and meaningful living can also influence the degree to which spirituality enters your day-to-day experience. This does not mean that you must read about hard-core religious rituals or dogma, but, rather, that it may be productive to read anything that can elevate your focus away from the typical magazine fodder of fashion, the latest gadgets, or celebrity gossip. Reading self-improvement books or discussions of world events with a human component also can be a form of spirituality that can lead you away from the common self-focus on getting rich or looking better.

You can choose from a vast array of experiences to enhance your life and strengthen your spiritual muscles. Activities such as yoga, meditation, connecting with the wonders of nature, or even volunteering to assist the disadvantaged, can elevate you to feel a deeper connection with others, and to your true inner self.

Taking inventory of how you spend your time, and what you focus on, can be eye-opening, and can help you become more open to pursuing a deeper, far richer personal life. Finally, choosing to experience life from a more spiritual plain, perhaps by attending a religious service or a spiritually-oriented group to reconnect, or connect for the first time, with your childhood spiritual heritage can be a deeply moving and meaningful experience that can help you open your heart to a life of new or renewed spirituality.

CASE EXAMPLE 26: KEVIN

Kevin was from a large, devout Catholic family. He grew up in a small suburb of Boston, where he attended a large parochial school. His strict, dogmatic father, a fireman, and his overwhelmed, often-depressed mother had little, if any, time or energy to provide the care or nurturing that Kevin desperately needed as a younger brother in a sea of boys who were all grappling for a slice of their parents' attention. The brother directly above him in age resented his very existence, and bullied him constantly. Some of the tougher boys in his class also bullied him. A priest in the school showed a special interest in him, and tried to provide him with the attention he obviously needed, and often took him on small outings to make him feel special. Adults often praised his religious practice and devotion, rewarding him with more attention and time. He enjoyed the attention and felt a connection with his faith that filled the void inside of him created by the emotional abyss in his family life.

Unfortunately, Kevin did not realize that this priest's special "attention" turned out to be grooming behaviors, which ended up in a steadily increasing pattern of sexual molestation. This caused Kevin tremendous distress and confusion, which eventually gave way to anger and betrayal, because he had thought that the priest genuinely cared for him, and that his interest was sincere and benevolent. When Kevin gathered the courage to speak to the school's headmaster about what was happening to him, the principal magnified his trauma, by launching a crushing attack accusing him of "making up things to get attention," and being "cursed by Satan." His grades, already on a steady decline, quickly plummeted, and he was soon expelled for his grave misdeeds and poor performance.

Kevin became an increasingly angry adolescent and young adult, and allowed his brooding resentments to spill over in all of his relationships, especially with his father, who represented everything he hated about religion and authority. He rebelled against the family's lifestyle, and rejected all the tenets of his faith, as well any attachment toward the church. He eventually detached from the family, and left for New York to find his way in a career in modeling, where his rugged good looks and sparkling, clear blue eyes helped him make quick money, and feed his insatiable ego as he pursued quick hookups with other models plus the finer things in life.

Kevin eventually moved to Miami, where he continued his quest to make it big as a fashion model on South Beach. Instead, he found himself in a vortex of drug and sex addiction that eventually derailed his life and career.

In therapy, he explored how he had allowed himself to get to such a point of chaos and desperation in his life. He eventually became in touch with the grief that he was feeling that was the catalyst for the need to anesthetize himself through drugs and compulsive sex. I referred him to Sex Addicts Anonymous, a 12-step program for recovering sex addicts, as well as to Father Lafferty, a local priest with whom I work here in Miami Beach. Father Lafferty cares for priests at a nearby church who are struggling with their sexuality. Kevin eventually reconnected with his religious roots, and realized that he had been numbing the pain of his early traumas at home and school through the highs of his addictive behaviors. He learned that he had been compensating for the resultant damage to his self-esteem by inflating his ego through endless sexual conquests and grandiose expenditures to feed his fragile ego.

He also realized that at a much deeper level he felt a sense of loss of the feeling of spiritual connection and belonging that he had felt in his early experiences in school, and that he actually longed for that attachment. He slowly began to reconnect to his faith through the efforts of Father Lafferty, who also helped him immeasurably to heal the narcissism that had plagued him for years. He left the modeling industry, entered an intensive outpatient addiction recovery program, and eventually went to college to become a physician's assistant. He married an attractive young former addict whom he met at a recovery weekend, and later became a sponsor who helped other recovering addicts. He has maintained his recovery ever since.

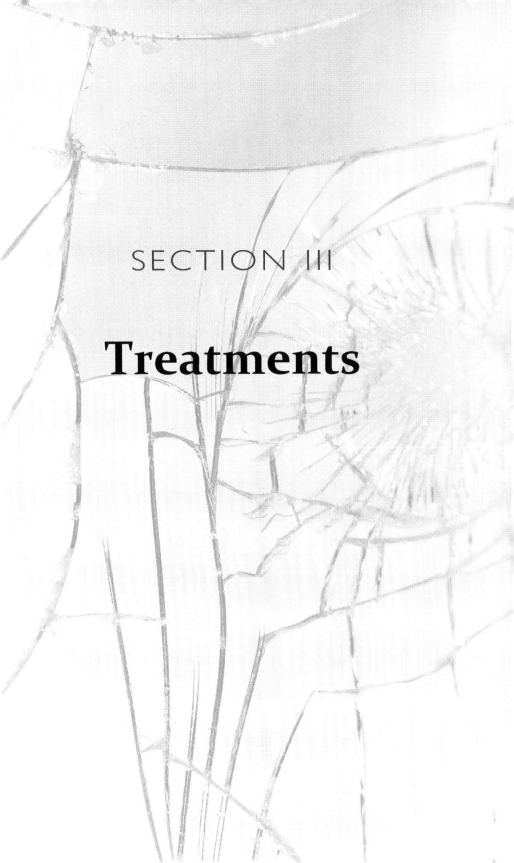

SECTION III

Treatments

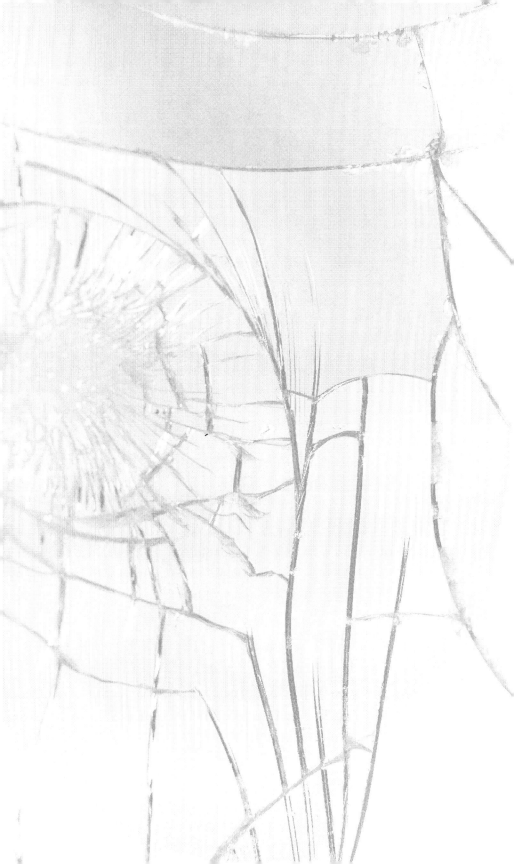

CHAPTER 13

But Therapy Doesn't Work for Me: Challenges to the Therapy Process

Defensiveness

Because of the fragile, weak ego and pervasive sense of inadequacy that often accompanies narcissism, people who are narcissistic commonly are defensive in their interactions with other people, especially when they are being challenged or called out for their behavior. This often plays out in therapy, at least initially, when a therapist begins to challenge the client, causing him or her to feel threatened, and triggering a defensive reaction. Defensiveness is a common reflex in narcissistic people, and it can make therapy challenging for both the client and the therapist. The ability to hear constructive feedback and to tolerate probing questions without being defensive or argumentative is an important part of the therapeutic process. It's a critical factor in reaching a successful outcome.

If you are in therapy or considering starting the therapeutic process, thinking through several points can help you avoid the pitfall of defensiveness in therapy.

First, and perhaps most importantly, remember that you are going for help to assist you in achieving important goals for yourself, and for your family—namely, the ability to be effective in all of your relationships, and to be more successful in your life in general. Being aware of this goal may help you to deal with challenging comments or face realities about yourself that may be difficult to handle.

Second, remember that your therapist is there to help you to achieve your important goals. To be effective in doing so, he or she will have to be able to confront your sometimes distorted thinking, point out how you are adversely affecting the people in your life, and challenge your perceptions about critical events that have occurred which may have damaged a relationship. This will ultimately help you see things from a different perspective. Allowing your therapist to accomplish all of this will help you enormously in reaching your therapeutic objectives.

Third, be consciously aware of the tendency to be defensive so you can vigilantly monitor your behavior and catch it on your own if you slip, and fall back into a pattern of defensiveness. You have developed strong neural pathways that influence well-worn patterns of narcissistic thinking and behavior, so you have to be more mindful and make a conscious effort to alter these maladaptive patterns of behavior.

Low Ego Strength

First described by Sigmund Freud in psychoanalytic theory, ego strength in this context refers to the ego's ability to deal effectively with the demands of the id, the superego, and reality. The id, according to Freud, is made up of all the primal urges and desires and is the only part of personality present at birth. The superego is the part of the personality composed of the internalized standards and rules that you acquire from your parents and society. It is the part of the personality that pressures people to behave morally. The ego, however, is the component of personality that mediates between the demands of reality, the urges of the id and the idealistic, but often unrealistic, standards of the superego.

While the id compels people to act on their most basic urges and the superego strives to achieve idealistic standards, the ego is the aspect of personality that must strike a balance among these baser urges, moral standards, and the demands of reality.

When it comes to well-being, "ego strength" is often used to describe individuals' ability to maintain their identity and sense of self in the face of challenge, distress, and conflict. This is vital for successful therapy, because ego strength is a critical prerequisite to being able to hear and accept what the therapist is trying to accomplish. A good therapist needs to give patients honest, straightforward feedback about their thinking, perceptions, or behavior, especially if that behavior undermines the building and maintaining of relationships.

Narcissistic clients often see this feedback as negative or critical. They can even feel betrayed by the therapist, especially if they think the clinician is, "taking the side" of the other person. These clients often get defensive or argumentative in response to candid feedback, because they are programmed to push back when criticized. However, if you can remember that therapy is a safe place, and that getting constructive feedback from a caring therapist is part of the process, you can increase your ego strength, handle the feedback with grace and maturity, and thereby derive maximum benefit from your therapist and the therapy process.

I can't count the number of clients who walked out of my office after being challenged about their behavior or thought processes, enraged and righteously indignant that I would have the gall to call them on their "stuff" instead of backing them up. They just couldn't handle the threat of being "wrong" or inappropriate. Instead of trying to hear what I was saying and to see things from the vantage point of the other person involved in the conflict, they projected the blame onto me for "not getting it" or not being loyal. Some of these patients were able to process their feelings and come back to work things out with me. However, others never returned.

They did not have sufficient ego strength to deal with the challenge from a therapist, regardless of the amount of the validity of the point, their established rapport, or the therapist's sincerity or communication skills. At some point, it doesn't really matter. The narcissistic ego is too fragile to handle the threat of being challenged, even by a trusted therapist.

CASE EXAMPLE 27: RICARDO

Luis's parents, Cuban immigrants who were very devout Catholics, brought him to therapy because he had "come out" to them, and disclosed that he was gay. Making matters worse in their eyes was learning that he was in a relationship with a fellow male student. The parents had come to see if I could help Luis, then 22, address their concerns about his sexual orientation. He was content, but they were not. After meeting with him, I could see that he was comfortable with his sexuality. His reasoning was sincere, authentic and mature. It was his parents, especially his father, Ricardo, who needed help to deal with Luis's reality and to accept him for who he is.

When I met privately with Ricardo, and his wife, Lourdes, who was quite sad and empathetic toward Luis' situation, I explained to them that Luis had worked hard to accept himself, and to be comfortable "in his own skin," and that he needed his parents' love and support to move forward with his life in a healthy and stable manner. I emphasized how vital it was that they work with him on this, as he had been suicidal in the past, and had stabilized, and was functioning rather well.

Ricardo became very agitated, and expressed outrage that I would expect them to accept something so abhorrent and against their religious beliefs and values. I gently challenged him that, as a 22-year-old adult, Luis had a right to live his life as he felt would work for him. I said they couldn't expect to force someone to change when he felt that this was a fixed reality for him. I added that, as much as it was difficult for them to accept this reality, a refined, honest, industrious young man such as Luis deserved his parents' love and support, and that without it, he could get depressed and suicidal once more.

When I directed my attention to Ricardo, and stressed how important it was for Luis to have the love of his father as he goes through these challenges, he flew into a rage. He yelled at me that I didn't know what I was talking about, and that they would take Luis to a "real doctor" who knew how to "fix" him. He grabbed his wife, and left the office, walking past Luis in the waiting room. As he watched his mother motioning him to come along with them, she broke down in tears.

I never heard from them again.

Ricardo was an unfortunate, sad example of a person who did not have the ego strength to deal with a threatening situation or to be challenged. He went into a rage when I challenged him to accept the situation and to love his son, despite his strong beliefs and values. His primitive anger and black-and-white thinking kept him from dealing with the reality of his son's pain and struggle.

Inability to Accept Responsibility

Within the context of therapy, the idea of taking personal responsibility is vital for a successful outcome. The person absolutely must "own" the therapy process as his or her work to do. The client must acknowledge that he or she must change to improve the quality of the relationship. Unless narcissistic people take responsibility, they usually blame everyone else for their problems. They focus on what is wrong with other people, instead of focusing on what they need to do to work on themselves. This allows them to avoid facing their flaws and personality defects, because that would be far too threatening for their weak egos to handle. Instead, they focus the blame for failed relationships on what's wrong with the other people.

To achieve your therapeutic goals, you need to walk into the first appointment with the conscious awareness that you have come in to work on yourself. That way you won't waste precious therapy time complaining about your spouse, your kids, your boss or your parents, or focusing on the degree to which you are a victim of their behavior. Try to resist the urge to do that, and muster the ego strength to face what you have done to alienate those around you. Begin by taking personal responsibility for whatever problems that exist in your relationships.

Once you can hold yourself accountable, you will be empowering yourself by working on the only person you really can control or change— yourself. Otherwise, you will continue to rail against the invariable frustration of trying to get others to change as you think they should. This will leave you feeling the utter powerlessness of realizing that you cannot change anyone else. And in the process, you'll waste precious time that you could otherwise use to work on yourself and deprive yourself of feeling the power of real personal change.

Defense Mechanisms

As we discussed in Chapter 7, people with narcissistic personalities use various defense mechanisms to protect themselves against their underlying feelings of inadequacy and defectiveness. These unconscious defenses, including denial, projection, displacement, and distortion, can also get in the way of succeeding in therapy and developing a healthy, collaborative relationship with a therapist. People who allow themselves to be in denial in the face of sincere, reality-based feedback from their therapists, or allow themselves to distort reality rather than face the difficult truths of how they have damaged their relationships, often get frustrated with the therapy process and drop out of therapy. They also tend to project blame on their therapists for not "being more supportive," or for not "getting it," and often displace their frustrations in life onto them, and vent their anger when challenged. They may project in the same way onto their spouses or children, further damaging their relationships.

Although seasoned therapists can process these reactions effectively with the patient, too often they never get the chance. The alienation that results from these dynamics—which may at times be mutual—can sabotage the therapeutic relationship, and can cause therapy to end in bitter disappointment and disillusionment. This can also lead to negative attitudes and pessimism about therapy in general, and keep people from ever trying to get help again.

Being aware of how these defense mechanisms can interfere with your progress in therapy is vital to your ability to succeed in the process. It is easy to blame your therapist for your frustrations or feelings of failures, as you may be blaming others in your life for your problems. However, if you can be aware of the patterns of these defense mechanisms in your day-to-day life, own up to them, and work with your therapist on avoiding them, you will undoubtedly have a more successful and rewarding outcome.

Transference and Counter-Transference

Transference is another Freudian concept that is relevant and related to the discussion above. It is generally translated as a redirection of emotions once generated and felt in childhood onto a current substitute figure, usually the therapist. Therapists often remind patients of a parent, a sibling, or another relative, and they attach strong feelings to the therapist based on the similarities that they experience. Negative transference refers to patients having uncomfortable or distressing feelings toward a therapist because of how they unconsciously relate to the clinician in association with past relationships. Teasing out and working through this dynamic can be very helpful in continuing a positive therapeutic relationship, and it can lead to significant personal growth.

Not all transference is negative, however. Positive transference refers to constructive feelings toward a therapist that help promote a positive therapeutic alliance. Feelings of trust, respect, and motivation to change can all contribute to a healthy therapeutic relationship. Whether these feelings represent underlying positive associations with earlier relationships in the patient's life, or just a reflection of good chemistry, having a comfortable, trusting relationship with your therapist can literally be life-changing. It can give you the opportunity to experience, perhaps for the first time in your life, a safe place to express your true feelings, to "bare your soul," in an environment that is non-judgmental, yet honest and straightforward.

Sometimes, working through negative transference, and making the transition to a relationship based primarily on positive transference is an important goal in therapy. A large part of the work—and the art of therapy—is to process through negative feelings and reactions in order to get to a better, more mature understanding of what caused the negative feelings. This can help the client develop a healthy attachment to the therapist.

That transformation, from a negatively tinged relationship based on past baggage to a more positive one based in the realities of the present can pave the way to experiencing trusting, loving relationships outside of the therapeutic environment in the future.

CASE EXAMPLE 28: NANCY

Having been raised by a deeply narcissistic mother who would rather be shopping than spending time with her family, and a deceitful, alcoholic father who gambled away his family's finances, and couldn't tell the truth about much of anything, Nancy had obvious trust issues. She was never able to develop a healthy attachment to anyone, much less an intimate partner. She felt early on in her life that, if she didn't take care of herself, no one else would. As a result, she developed into a self-absorbed, untrusting person who kept people at a distance and had difficulty with her work relationships.

I was a consultant and Employee Assistance provider in the company where Nancy worked in the accounting department. The owner referred her to me because of the difficulties her co-workers were having with her, even though she was a good performer. Specifically, she was hypersensitive to any feedback, even that which was basically positive. This resulted in a tense, difficult relationship with her direct supervisor. She was also seen as a poor team member because she had difficulty sharing information or assisting her co-workers when they needed help with something in her area.

At first, Nancy was clear that she had no interest in coming to see me, and that she came only because the owner asked her to. She told me at the outset that she didn't trust psychologists, and they were all nosy, annoying people who "want to get into your business."

"What fun!", I thought to myself, and checked my counter-transference meter. It was running high—I definitely was uncomfortable being with her, and it was quite clear that the feelings were mutual. However, after we spent some time trying to explore how she could improve her relationships with the people in her department, she realized that she had a lot to gain by trying to work on her personal baggage so she could deal with people more effectively. She also realized that I genuinely cared about her and her ability to succeed, because she was quite capable and much needed by her company for the diligent work that she was doing. Her feelings gradually softened toward me, as well, and she gradually developed a healthy attachment that helped pave her way to the possibility of opening up to one or two people in her department who had tried to be nice to her. Eventually, she had changed to the point that she was named Employee of the Month, after being nominated by her supervisor, who wanted to recognize her efforts to work on herself and her relationships with her colleagues.

CHAPTER 14

What Do I Want to Accomplish? Goals of Therapy

Healthy, Stable Relationships

As we discussed in Chapter 10, narcissism has a profound and pervasive effect on your ability to attain and sustain relationships. The lack of mutuality and balance, difficulty in communicating, the sense of entitlement, difficulty being intimate, and parenting issues, all take their toll on relationships with spouses or partners, children, other relatives, friends, and people at work. The bottom line is that if you have narcissistic features in your personality, and you relate to at least some of what you have read so far, it's very likely that you are having problems with at least some of your relationships.

The most important goals in your therapy should include achieving the ability to develop healthier, more meaningful relationships and becoming able to get along better with other people. Many of the people with whom I have worked with over the years found that therapy helped them to reduce or avoid conflict in their marriages and with their children, parents, siblings, and colleagues. As a result, they feel less isolated and victimized, and generally more satisfied with their lives.

Another important aspect of therapy is to work on the stability of your relationships. Many people with narcissistic personalities find that their relationships are stormy, with a lot of drama, since they tend to be more sensitive, more easily triggered, and more triggering of the people in their lives. Those who work hard in therapy to be less hypersensitive and reactive find that their relationships become smoother and less complicated, resulting in lives that are less stressful and upsetting. Letting go of the tendency to be slighted or hurt by the imperfections of those around us leads to greater stability in our relationships and less time spent in wounded, angry emotional states. The benefits of this calmer, more stable way of living, in terms of emotional and physical well-being, are boundless.

CASE EXAMPLE 29—KENNY

A perennial bachelor, Kenny was a 41-year-old executive in his family's successful insurance company. By his own report, he had never had a "real" relationship, but had a multitude of short flings with highly attractive, model-type women, interspersed with sexual encounters with high-priced escorts. Although he had some drinking buddies, and a few golf partners, he didn't have any real "friends," and he found that people often distanced themselves from him after a while, leaving him to find new people to hang out with. His relationships at work were problematic, as a result of his careless and often irresponsible behavior, which too frequently caused problems with clients that his disgruntled employees had to fix. They saw him as an entitled, spoiled trust-fund baby who rested on the laurels of the hard work of his father and grandfather who had built up the business over many years. Unlike them, he did not appear to feel the need to work hard. Instead, he preferred to travel all over the world or to spend time at local social events, ostensibly to "build up business."

Kenny came into therapy with his father, Leo, who initiated the contact because of his frustration with his son's poor work ethic, complaints by his staff, and concern that his son would be alone the rest of his life as a result of his inability to attain a meaningful relationship. Kenny also had a stormy relationship with his brother, Frank, who also worked at the business, but was a work horse and resented Kenny's lack of discipline and drive. Kenny was never raised with an awareness of limits—as a result of a lack of active involvement in his development by his parents, who were very busy in the family business—he was unable to function within a healthy, mature relationship, either personally or professionally.

Over the period of time that Kenny was in therapy, he slowly realized that his life was going nowhere, and that he ran the risk of being alone and miserable for the rest of his life, unless he worked on his ability to succeed in a relationship. He also allowed me to mentor him in regard to how he functioned at work, to participate in team meetings, and to get to know the staff and how they felt about his personality and work style. We developed corrective action plans to improve his work performance and relationships with his staff, and he became more responsive and respectful toward them. Over time, he gradually earned their respect, as well.

He also agreed to stop engaging in relationships with models and escorts, and to date only women with whom he saw some potential for a long-term relationship. Through a business contact, he met a woman who was quite different from the women he used to date. An accomplished musician with an advanced degree from an Ivy League school, Tory was the opposite of what Kenny was accustomed to, but he was attracted to her personality, which was warm and subdued, and not flashy and demanding like the models he had dated. She understood and accepted Kenny's challenges, and saw that he did have a good heart that was beginning to emerge. Eventually, they married, and they started a family shortly thereafter.

Self-Esteem

As we discussed in Chapter 3, many people who have narcissism in their personalities were damaged early in their development by trauma, abuse, and neglect, and as a result, suffered significant blows to their self-esteem. Narcissism, as has been frequently mentioned, is a defensive reaction to underlying feelings of inadequacy and defectiveness that developed as a result of experiences in earlier years of life. When you are ignored, abused, wounded, or traumatized in your early relationships, it is difficult to feel any self-worth or to have much self-esteem.

One of the most important earlier goals of any therapy process is to come to feel better about yourself. A kind, supportive, and empowering therapist, who can balance the ability to call you out on your "stuff" and to build up your confidence and self-worth by focusing on your strengths and assets, can enhance your self-esteem immeasurably. Many people with narcissistic personalities never had anyone in their lives who made the effort or took the time (or cared enough) to compliment them or to focus on what is good about them. Quite often, they were raised by narcissistic parents or had siblings who were narcissistic who put them down when they were growing up. Or they may have been the victims of bullying at school. They were given the very clear message that they were inadequate or defective and that they weren't worth much.

A good therapy experience can help you feel better about yourself by focusing on what is right about you, where you excel, and your innate goodness, as well as working hard on the areas of your personality that don't work too well. An experienced, confident therapist will know how and when to build you up, and also how and when to challenge you when you are out of line. As you develop better relationship skills, you will likely find that your relationships improve. When you see that people are responding to you differently, it's only natural that you will start to feel better about yourself.

Increased Achievement and Accomplishments

One of the things that I have experienced over the years of working with people who are trying to work on their personalities, is that the effects of therapy can generalize to all aspects of your life. Many patients who come in to address a troubled marriage or difficulty with their children report back to me that, over time, their relationships and performance at work somehow improve as well. This is not difficult to understand, because all of our work life or career usually involves relationships. Most of us, unless you are a computer geek who sits behind a monitor all day, interact with people during the course of day or, more likely, depend on an ability to deal effectively with people in order to succeed in our jobs.

A patient of mine from Australia reported to me that his direct supervisor is a petulant woman who is deeply insecure in her managerial role, undermines her subordinates whenever possible, and only knows how to criticize. She hasn't a clue about the need to pay a compliment once in a while. Over time, as more and more employees made transfer requests to be moved off of her team and complained about her treatment of them, upper management began to take notice, and eventually put her on probationary status. Instead of taking the feedback in a constructive, professional manner, she reacted strongly by protesting the action and threatening to take legal action for gender discrimination. She was eventually fired, and had to take a job as a department store saleswoman, because no one in her field would hire her after her dismissal. Yes, Virginia, relationship skills do matter.

Whether or not you come in for therapy specifically to work on your job performance or career advancement, if you work on your personality and try to enhance your people skills for any reason, you will invariably improve your ability to achieve. Even if you enter therapy following a divorce that was caused, to some extent, by your personality, you have a lot to benefit from in all areas of your life if you focus on becoming, in general, a more humble, other-centered person.

CASE EXAMPLE 30: JON

Jon, and his wife, Leeanne, came in to see me because she discovered that he had been in an affair with a client for whom he had worked as a financial advisor. Jon came from an unstable home, in which his parents were more focused on their disdain for each other than on the needs of their children. They eventually divorced, which was highly adversarial and traumatizing for Jon and his siblings. Jon was left with a badly damaged sense of self. He had underlying feelings of worthlessness as a result of the emotional neglect that he experienced from his parents who were too busy fighting to take care of and be supportive of Jon and his siblings. This dynamic led to Jon's development of a narcissistic personality to defend against these feelings of worthlessness.

When they first came in for treatment, Jon was obviously highly narcissistic, showing no remorse for his behavior, and blaming Leanne for not being more sexually available and for being too critical of him. He was grandiose and spoke frequently about how wealthy his high-profile clients were, and how they had made him into a wealthy man, as well. He often would spout on about various issues, presenting himself as the expert who needed to be admired and adhered to, in every way, while Leanne would sit there, cringing at his obvious boorishness and lack of self-awareness.

Over time, and with a lot of feedback and challenging of his aversive behaviors, Jon began to be more aware of how negatively he was affecting his wife and others in his life, and he gradually became more humble and contrite. His involvement in a therapy group for narcissistic men (more about that later) also contributed significantly to his healing and growth, due to getting feedback from the other men, but also due to seeing the narcissism in them, and realizing that he didn't want to be like that anymore. Eventually, his personality changed considerably, and he became much more likeable and easier to connect with. His native intelligence and innate good will began to emerge, and he became much kinder and other-centered. Even though Jon and Leanne eventually divorced, they were able to achieve a collaborative divorce, and continue to cooperate and to work together to co-parent their children as a team with no tension or acrimony.

What was striking about Jon's transition out of narcissism was that he noticed that his business began to pick up, and that he was being referred more and more clients from a variety of sources. He also became aware that the quality of the relationships that he had with his clients became more rich and multifaceted, to the point that he had received quite a bit of feedback from his co-workers, as well as clients, about how much they had seen him change over the year, and how much more pleasant and enjoyable it was to be with him. At the end of the year, he reported to me that his accountant told him that his earnings had increased by almost a third from the previous year. He attributed this accomplishment solely to the work that he had done in therapy, which was only supposed to be focused on the crisis in his marriage, and his relationship with his wife. It turned out that when he worked on his personality, all of his relationships improved significantly, as did his ability to achieve in his career.

Greater Clarity: Self-Awareness and Insight

Most people who are involved with narcissists experience them as being "clueless" about themselves and how they affect other people. The defenses of distortion and denial, discussed at length in Chapter 7, keep them hopelessly oblivious to the reality of their situation, that they are not as loveable as they think, and that they are, in fact, quite aversive and disliked by many of the people around them. Those who are grandiose have a very distorted self-concept of being wildly successful and admired, when, in fact, they are not nearly as accomplished as they think.

In reality, they lack the clarity to be congruent with the perceptions that others have of them. This lack of clarity often causes them to misfire in situations that call for clearheaded good judgment and to make mistakes that alienate other people. Therapy can be an excellent venue for getting genuine, accurate feedback from a caring therapist about what is going on in your life and how you are really affecting the people around you.

One of the therapeutic approaches in which I was trained while I was in graduate school is called Interpersonal Communications Theory, first developed by Harry Stack Sullivan in the 1960s. My clinical supervisor, Dr. Donald Kiesler, was an extraordinarily gifted therapist who, in many ways, was the person who was most influential in helping me to develop me as a therapist. Sullivan trained Don, whose therapeutic style reflected Sullivan's influence, since Don—and then I—integrated it into our own approach to therapy. This approach is based on the premise that people can grow and develop their ability to have successful relationships only if they get honest feedback in therapy as to how they are affecting the therapist. This can provide invaluable, priceless awareness of how they affect other people. I have experienced patients who had never, in their entire lives, received honest feedback about their behavior and impact on others, primarily because they intimidated the people around them, who were uncomfortable or afraid to be completely honest about how they truly felt about them. Therapy can be that opportunity to gain clarity and awareness of what is really happening in your life, as opposed to what you want to believe is happening.

One of the more enlightened patients whom I've seen told me after almost a year of therapy that he never imagined that being told how negatively he was affecting me, his therapist—and sometimes in more detail that he would have preferred—would be a life-changing experience for him. Because we had eventually developed a strong rapport after a bit of a rough start (to say the least), he trusted what I had said to him about his behavior and how it had affected me. He came to realize that what he heard from me rang true, in terms of things that he had heard from his wife and children, as well as other people.

He began, over time, to be more aware of his interpersonal impact, and he was successful in changing the way that he related to others. He became much more humble, and tried harder to listen to what others were saying, without being defensive or argumentative. He let go of the need to be right and was able to see that the other person had a perspective that may have had some merit, as well. His relationships gradually improved over time, as did his self-concept and how he felt about himself. All of this occurred because his therapist found the strength to tell him the truth about how he was affecting him, and that he was likely affecting others in his life in a similar manner. That was the pivotal factor that caused him to look in the mirror, and to change himself, which ended up changing his life.

Integrity

Oftentimes, people with narcissistic personalities compromise their personal integrity in ways that are not always readily apparent. They can be manipulative and deceitful to get their way or to get their needs met. They frequently can alter facts in order to get out of situations where they got themselves into trouble because of their narcissistic behavior. They also distort reality, as we discussed in Chapter 7, in ways to defend themselves, which, in its own way, is a way in which personal integrity is compromised.

This dynamic can be further compounded and exacerbated when you are also dealing with an addiction. As was discussed in Chapter 6, narcissism often contributes to and maintains addictive behaviors, in a number of ways. The feelings of pain and shame, which often underlie narcissistic personalities, can lead to the need to anaesthetize those feelings with drugs, alcohol, sex, food, gambling, or the drama of an affair. This allows a person to disconnect from their inner reality and to drown their pain with addictive behavior. Addictions usually involve a sense of entitlement to indulge in the behavior, for a variety of reasons, including not being understood or treated well enough by one's partner, because they are special, and therefore are entitled to do what they want, or because they have had a hard life, and therefore deserve to have a "break" every once in a while.

Addictions invariably cause a person to lie, deceive, or manipulate to maintain the addictive behavior. Addicts usually develop sociopathy, which involves lies, manipulation, and exploitation, in order to maintain their addiction. To continue addictive behavior, addicts have to lie to those who are close to them to keep from exposing the secret of their addiction. Eventually, they develop the pattern of lying and deceiving that eventually infects their personality. It becomes part of the fabric of who they are as people and how they relate to others. Therapy is critical to uncover these personality dynamics and to develop new patterns of interpersonal behavior based on honesty and integrity.

When working with a therapist who is, on the one hand, strong enough to call you on your "stuff" to hold you accountable for your lack of genuine behavior and, on the other hand, caring enough to tell you how you can be more successful, a lot can happen in terms of you becoming a person who is more effective and has more integrity. By being called out when you try to manipulate the people—including your therapist, for that matter—you can start to redirect yourself toward being more rigorously honest. It also forces you to be in reality, and stay there, instead of manipulating yourself into believing things that are simply not true, just to protect your own ego.

Eventually, therapy can allow you to experience more respect for yourself, which can contribute in healing the wounds that caused you to be narcissistic in the first place. Learning and practicing to live with integrity can be a tremendous boost to your self-esteem, and to develop a healthier self-concept as a fundamentally honest person, who tries to be straight and honest in all of your relationships. It can also substantially improve these relationships by helping the people in your lives to feel that they are dealing with someone who is actually being honest and straightforward with them, instead of making them feeling manipulated and deceived. By helping you to become more honest with others, as well as yourself, you can allow therapy to help you transform yourself into someone who people would actually want to have a relationship with, and eventually grow to like—or love.

Emotional Stability

It is often the case that narcissistic people tend to be emotionally unstable, whose relationships are equally unstable, as well. Intense emotions, hypersensitivity, angry reactions, and difficulty regulating or modulating emotions all can contribute to a general pattern of instability. This pattern of heightened emotions can be physically, as well as emotionally exhausting, and can often lead to depression, especially when there is a lot of victimization and self-pity.

An important goal of therapy is to learn how not to get so triggered, and to manage your emotional reactions when you do get triggered. From a behavioral perspective, there are numerous anger management strategies that can be beneficial to keep you from losing it when you are in a situation that would normally trigger you to react strongly. The ultimate goal, however, would be to heal at a deeper level, so that you just don't get triggered the way that you used to, or not at all.

People who have been wounded or traumatized as children often have highly triggerable nervous systems, and are more likely to be more emotionally reactive, and to react more strongly than those who were not abused or mistreated. Well-developed neural pathways that emanated from traumatic experiences are entrenched within our brains, and fire off vigorously when a situation that we experience in the present is in any way associated with previous traumatic experiences. So, for example, if you are being given feedback about how you acted in a way that affected someone negatively, instead of calmly taking it in, and realizing that it is for your own benefit, the old neural pathways of anger and shame that developed from earlier emotional abuse gets triggered, and you will likely react with the same intensity of rage and shame that you felt when you were much younger. This is the dynamic that underlies Post-Traumatic Stress Disorder (PTSD), as described in Chapter 6, and, if properly treated, can greatly contribute to a greater healing of your narcissistic personality features. This, in turn, can lead to a greater sense of calmness and serenity, which invariably can lead to greater emotional stability, in general.

Physical Well-Being

As mentioned earlier, being emotionally intense, hypersensitive, easily triggered, and often angry, can be physically exhausting, and quite depleting. Life can be draining for a narcissist because of the constant upset and drama, and this can take a toll on physical well-being. Stress-related disorders, which are not uncommon in people with these personality features, can include headaches, high blood pressure, fibromyalgia, and neuralgia, and can have serious deleterious effects on one's life.

Some people who have narcissistic personalities become what is termed clinically as highly "somaticized." This means that they internalize their emotional problems in a way that their bodies are affected by their emotions. They often have a wide array of physical ailments, and spend an inordinate amount of time focusing on what ails them, often in great detail, and *ad nauseum*. This often results from, and feeds into, their incessant need for attention, which paradoxically they are less likely to receive because other people usually get tired of all of the complaints and the person's litany of symptoms. This is different from hypochondriasis, in which people genuinely think that there is something wrong with them, when, in truth, they are fine, since somaticized people may have genuine issues with their bodies. It's also unlike a person who is malingering, which involves more deliberate "faking," and is a more, conscious, blatant attempt to manipulate or exploit.

Therapy can be very helpful in uncovering these dynamics, and can help people understand the role that their symptoms play in their personality, as well as what secondary gains they are accomplishing through being sick. A side benefit of psychotherapy is that, if you can achieve a healing of your personality, you can also accomplish a calmer disposition that can create an overall feeling of wellness from a physical perspective. If you are less triggered, and less triggerable in general, your body will most likely become less tense, more relaxed, and less affected by the stress that you previously experienced. This can undoubtedly create a new equilibrium in your nervous system that will help your body to heal and to improve your general health.

The mind-body relationship is important to consider here, as the effect of chronic emotional upset on the body has been well established. So, it goes to follow that if you calm your mind, you will calm your body as well. Therapy can help your mind become calmer and more relaxed, ease the tension in your nervous system, and allow for a greater sense of well-being in general. Combined with a general wellness program, which can include a regiment of exercise, proper nutrition, complementary supplements, mindfulness, yoga, and meditation, among other steps, psychotherapy can lead to a greatly enhanced immune system, less probability of disease, and a generally enhanced sense of physical wellness.

CASE EXAMPLE 31: GLORIA

Having lost her husband several years ago, Gloria had spent much of her time since that loss desperately searching for solutions to the myriad of health problems that she had been experiencing, some since her husband's death and others which had preceded it. She had been diagnosed with fibromyalgia, and often experienced debilitating pain throughout her body, as well as migraines, which would leave her completely immobilized. She was also convinced that she had chronic fatigue syndrome, although no clinical test data could confirm that. This was all on top of various dental issues, skin problems, digestive issues, and problems with her feet, all of which kept her going from one doctor's appointment to another, as well as visiting to alternative practitioners on an endless search for the elusive cure of one ailment or another.

Gloria's two daughters were expected to endure a daily dose of hearing about what ailed her, and what happened during the last doctor's visit, as well as a tongue lashing about not being available to take her to the latest appointment. One of her daughters, Lisa, was advised by her own therapist to stop all contact with her mother because it had become toxic to her, both emotionally and physically. The stress had taken its toll on her and her ability to cope with her own parenting and marital stresses. Lisa's decision to cut herself off from her mother prompted Gloria to come in for help.

From the initial visit with Gloria, a strikingly beautiful blonde with sparklingly clear blue eyes, it became apparent that she had grown up in an emotionally impoverished environment. Her mother was diagnosed with Borderline Personality Disorder, and was both emotionally abusive and unavailable, and her father was an alcoholic who spent most days at work and most evenings out drinking. As an only child, she had no one to turn to for help or comfort. Even her maternal grandmother, who lived with them, was mean and critical of her because she was jealous of Gloria's youth and beauty. Gloria gradually realized that the only times that she was able to get attention from anyone were when she was sick. She was often in the nurse's office at school because of stomach issues, headaches, and various muscle strains, which enabled her to spend time with the nurse, who was kind and attentive. Otherwise, she was on her own—expected to fend for herself, with little or no support from her family.

Although Gloria's insight into her relationship difficulties with her daughters, as well as her obsessive preoccupation with her health, was limited, she gradually began to understand through the therapy process that she was overburdening her family with her constant complaints and need for attention. Family therapy with her daughters opened up a dialogue about boundaries and limits, and her daughters expressed the desire to have a relationship with her, but one that was based on these types of parameters. Gloria also started to understand how her ailments were an unconscious need for attention. Although she still maintained that her symptoms were real, she started to defocus away from them, and looked into wellness retreats that offered holistic approaches to healing that incorporated mind-body perspectives to wellness. Eventually, as she relaxed the demands for attention and unreasonable expectations of her daughters, she found that some of her physical symptoms subsided, and she gradually began to be at peace with her family—and with herself.

Inner Peace

If, as a result of a successful therapy experience, you are less prone to anger, can accept people for who they are, have healthier and more satisfying relationships, and have a stronger sense of self-worth and physical well-being, it is likely that you will also be able to attain a greater sense of inner peace, as well. This, in my view, is defined as an internal sense of "okness"—I am OK, you are OK, and the world is good. It occurs when you feel an sense of equilibrium, that your world is in order, and you have a general feeling of peace most of the time. No one, unless you are a monk in a monastery in Tibet, achieves inner peace all of the time, but if you can feel it most of the time, or even some of the time, then you can feel content with the world—and with yourself.

Inner peace is not easily accomplished or achieved overnight. Attaining it can be a lifetime struggle, to be sure, but being in therapy with someone who can help you to heal your wounds also can help you achieve greater self-awareness and self-acceptance. This can assist you in healing and enhancing your relationships, which can lead to inner peace. This is certainly an achievable goal that is definitely worth the effort it will require.

Inner peace can enable you to accept what you can't change about others or yourself. Acceptance of the realities of your life, and whatever limitations or disappointments you may have experienced, is the real key to the acquiring of inner peace. In my mind, it related very closely to the concept of serenity, as described in the "Serenity Prayer," espoused by 12-step programs such as Alcoholics Anonymous:

G-d grant me the serenity
to accept the things I cannot change;
courage to change the things I can;
and wisdom to know the difference.

Spiritual Openness

As was discussed in Chapter 12, narcissism often affects your ability to experience a true sense of spirituality. Narcissistic people are often more likely to leave the faith of their upbringing, reject their family's religious values and traditions, and feel a general sense of spiritually emptiness. They may have conflicts with their spouse in terms of lifestyle and religious affiliation and practice, since they may no longer wish to be controlled by rituals or laws and feel no real connection to G-d or a higher power. Often, their sole focus in life is to get their needs met, to achieve greatness or power, and to be financially successful. Spiritual growth is not usually on the radar screen of a true narcissist, and if they are outwardly religious, it is likely that it is for external purposes only, and to show a certain image for public display.

Oftentimes, the root cause of the narcissism is related to early aversive or traumatic experiences associated with religion. Heavy-handed religious instruction, dogmatic religious ideas, or restrictive lifestyle requirements, without the requisite balance of love and respect, can often lead to resentment and the feeling of being controlled, diminished, or abused. These experiences often, if not usually, result in alienation from religious life, and spirituality, in general. Anything associated with religion becomes aversive and something to be avoided or rejected.

As you heal as a result of the experience of therapy—especially if members of your family of origin who may have contributed to your religious alienation are involved in the therapeutic process—you may find that a new openness to spiritually emerges, and that you are more willing to engage in discussions about a higher level of existence, other than material possessions, superficial experiences, or financial accomplishments. As we discussed in Chapter 12, spirituality can take a wide variety of forms, and how you relate to spirituality may be unique to your personality and personal experience. How you connect, or reconnect if you once had a spiritual connection, will depend on many factors, most importantly what speaks to your heart, or, perhaps more pertinently, to your soul.

CASE EXAMPLE 32: LEVI

Levi was a 26-year-old from an ultra-Orthodox Jewish home in Brooklyn. In his late teens, he adopted a different lifestyle than his family. He stopped all forms of religious observance, started dating a Catholic girl from Spain, and had minimal contact with his family. His experience with religious observance was one of fear and intimidation, as his school was run in a strict, authoritarian manner by a principal who would use shame and corporal punishment as a means of discipline and religious direction. His parents were impotent in dealing with the situation, preferring to back up the school, for fear of being labeled as having questionable religious standing. Levi deeply resented this and when it came to parenting and protecting himself and his siblings, "no one was home," as he caustically put it.

Levi developed strong narcissistic traits which manifested in grandiose schemes that invariably ended up with him getting in some sort of trouble. His relentless goal was to be fabulously wealthy, and he tried many ways to reach this goal through "get rich quick" schemes that turned sour. Levi used his unusual good looks to bring in money, often through modeling gigs, but also by being hired out as an escort by wealthy women. His relationships with other women also were superficial and exploitive. He dated only women with money who could "take care of him."

He presented for treatment because he had also developed another problem—cocaine. His drug habit had gotten out of control, and he was referred to me by another patient who had recovered from sex addiction through therapy and a 12-step program. What struck me about Levi was that, although he was entrenched in a high-flying South Beach lifestyle, part of him grieved the loss of his family and aspects of the lifestyle he once led.

As much as he hated his religious upbringing, there was still very much something stirring inside of him that missed home.

Once he had reached a point in therapy that he understood what had happened to him, and how his personality had been affected by his early experiences, we were ready for a family intervention. His parents and two of his once closest siblings flew down to Florida to meet with Levi and to make an attempt at some sort of reconciliation, which ended up being successful. It was a deeply moving, emotional experience for Levi, as he reconnected to the warmth and genuineness of his family's love for him, and it helped him overcome his addiction and heal the wounds that had damaged him so greatly. He started to gravitate towards a Rabbi near where he lived in South Beach. The Rabbi embraced him and helped him connect with a more authentic, embracing brand of Judaism than the one that he had rejected years ago.

Life Satisfaction

Over the years, the thing that I have found most often in working with patients who have been wounded or neglected as children, and, as a result, developed narcissistic personalities, is that they are generally not satisfied in their lives. They are often bitter, resentful, jealous, upset, and just plain miserable. They spend much of the time dwelling on things that people have done to them, what they want that they don't have, how others have ignored them, and comparing other people's success or assets to their own, and dwelling on how basically unfair things are.

On the other hand, the most gratifying experiences that I have had as a therapist are when I am able to witness patients, through the arduous process of psychotherapy, transform from being bitter, resentful person to being able to feel real gratitude and joy for what life can offer. When you can learn how to develop and benefit from healthy relationships, enhance your self-esteem, achieve more in your in life, and when you have more self-awareness and insight, operate with more integrity, become more emotionally stable, feel better physically, experience inner peace, and feel more connected spiritually, you will undoubtedly feel more joyous and satisfied with your life.

Life satisfaction has been correlated with physical health, emotional well-being, occupational success, and positive relationships. It can help you to feel the inner peace and serenity discussed above. It is facilitated by mindful awareness and conscious gratitude, which comes about when you have used therapy to eliminate, or greatly reduce the narcissistic aspects of your personality. Being mindfully aware of what you have to be grateful for is a key element that can lead to being satisfied with your life and to being at peace with yourself.

Life satisfaction is a precious gift that should not be underestimated. To be satisfied with how your life is going, and how you are living it, is a goal that may be the most important thing that you can achieve. To experience true joy and satisfaction for a life well-lived is a definitely achievable goal. Once you have gone through the process of healing through therapy, you can develop the insight and the tools to achieve successful relationships, both with others as well as yourself. When you have accomplished that, you have found the key to breaking the mirror, and then, anything and everything is possible.

CHAPTER 15

How to Get There:
Individual Therapies

Psychodynamic Psychotherapies

Traditional psychotherapy developed from the psychoanalytic school of psychology. It focuses on Freudian concepts such as unconscious conflicts, defense mechanisms, and early childhood experiences that shaped your personality. In psychoanalysis, the therapist facilitates your efforts to reach a deeper understanding of the process that influenced the development of your personality, and helps you uncover layers of defenses that you may be using to protect your fragile ego. One goal is to develop a "superego" or a moral conscience that can guide you to have a greater degree of personal balance and a higher level of relationships.

This type of therapy requires a serious commitment on your part to engage in an intense journey of analysis and self-discovery. Sessions are typically held several times a week, and psychoanalysis can last for many years. The process is highly structured, and the analyst often behaves passively since the preferred mode of therapy is to allow the patient to search and explore the deeper chambers of his unconscious. The analyst's role is to gently probe and prod the patient with interpretations and suggestions for further exploration of hidden meanings and insight into unconscious conflicts and processes.

Less orthodox methods of psychotherapy are generally referred to as psychodynamic, or insight-oriented, therapy. Less strict and structured than psychoanalysis, such therapies are oriented toward assisting patients in connecting the dots of what happened in their childhood. Therapy explores how childhood events affected the formation of their person-ality and potentially led to the development of their current problems. Psychodynamic therapy helps patients develop insight into the ways they function (or malfunction) and to achieve a deeper understanding of how to manage their life in an emotionally healthier, more effective way.

Psychodynamic therapists tend to adhere less rigidly to a specific approach, and they can be more eclectic in their therapeutic style. Even though their training may have emanated from the psychoanalytic tradi-tion, they often branch out beyond the strict interpretation of Freudian theory and practice. They may embrace a wider range of therapeutic tech-niques that address a broader view of the patient's life. Insight-oriented therapists are often trained in a wide range of different therapies which may coalesce under the umbrella of psychodynamic psychotherapy. They actually can depart considerably from a strict psychoanalytical traditional approach and be far more eclectic in actual clinical practice.

Psychodynamic therapies, regardless of which flavor you choose, can help you understand some of the root causes of the damage to your per-sonality and how you developed into the person you are today. They can also help you identify the various defense mechanisms you use to defend yourself when you feel threatened. Your goal is to develop a healthier, more mature, evolved ego that doesn't need to employ defenses to com-pensate for fragility or insecurity. Therapy also can help you develop new, healthier ways of relating to others and can make you more aware of the unconscious processes that previously derailed you and your relationships.

Cognitive-Behavioral Therapy

B.F. Skinner's work on behavioral conditioning in the 1940s involved modifying behavioral responses to specific stimuli. This work evolved into cognitive-behavioral therapy (CBT), which was developed by theorists such as Aaron Beck, Albert Ellis, and Donald Meichenbaum, who felt that strictly defined behavioral therapies were too radical a departure from psychoanalysis. They also found that these approaches didn't incorporate the profound behavioral influence of internal, cognitive processes—that is, the impact of individual thinking on the way people act—beyond just the basic stimulus-response mechanism.

Cognitive therapists can help you to look at your thought processes and identify maladaptive or negative thought patterns that may be contributing to your problems. Therapy helps you identify irrational thought patterns, often called "cognitive distortions," and introduces alternate ways of thinking to gradually replace irrational ideas.

Over time, a good therapist can teach you to think in a way that reflects the reality of your situation, instead of allowing your emotions to influence what you perceive. The therapist can also assist you in preserving your self-esteem by helping you to avoid personalizing negative events or your experience with toxic people.

A competent, strong therapist can also challenge your thinking if you have a tendency to see yourself as a victim. The therapist could point out how your behavior may have contributed to a problem and could help you hold yourself responsible for your part. Taking personal responsibility is critical in your journey toward transitioning out of a narcissistic personality.

CBT calls for individually tailored treatment plans in order to focus on and achieve specific therapeutic goals. Thus, CBT is a more structured, time-limited strategy rather than the more flexible, open-ended approach of psychodynamic therapy. The objective of CBT is to move you out of therapy once you've achieved your goals. CBT therapists also tend to focus on specific skills to enhance general functioning. These skills-training models can help you develop necessary skills of effective living if you didn't develop them in childhood.

Dialectic Behavioral Therapy

Dialectic Behavior Therapy (DBT) is an adaptation of CBT that focuses on reinforcing the skills you need to deal with problems associated with Borderline Personality Disorder (BPD). Narcissism and Borderline

Personality Disorder share common problems and overlapping symptoms. Therefore, DBT can be very effective in helping patients overcome problems associated with narcissism as well.

This therapy program focuses on four basic skills that are seen as being critical to healthy emotional and interpersonal functioning. These are:

1. **Mindfulness**—This refers to the ability to be mindfully aware of what is going on at any given time, instead of mindlessly reacting to a given situation. Mindfulness enables you to be more thought-driven, instead of emotion-driven, and to *respond* to the person with whom you are interacting, rather than being *reactive.* A person who responds is actively thinking about the best approach to take and trying to focus on the other person. When you are reactive, you're experiencing an emotional reflex and you're probably not thinking about what the other person is experiencing or needs to hear in order to respond back to you effectively. Mindfulness is the key to being aware and to responding to a challenging situation in an effective way. DBT can help you develop mindfulness as a tool that can strengthen your ability to be other-centered. It can help you become more aware of the needs, feelings, and unique sensitivities of the other person, instead of being focused on yourself and what you need.

2. **Stress Tolerance**—Stress is a normal experience. The way you deal with it depends on your skills and ability to manage it effectively. Your stress management skills greatly influence your ability to remain emotionally stable and effective in dealing with life's normal challenges. Narcissism often affects your ability to manage stress, since it interferes with clear, calm thinking. The narcissistic personality's hypersensitivity often triggers strong emotional reactions. As noted, narcissism often can make you to feel as if you are a victim, which can disempower you and keep you from developing strategies for dealing with stress. DBT can help you separate emotionally from ongoing stress and develop ways to deal with it that can keep you emotionally stable and feeling effective and empowered.

3. Emotional Regulation—The inability to manage or regulate your emotions is a hallmark of Borderline Personality Disorder and a common challenge of narcissistic people as well. People with narcissism often are very emotional, which is not surprising given the trauma and damage they often endured in their earlier, formative years, when their personalities were being shaped. Being emotionally reactive can affect you in many ways, as we previously discussed in Chapter 9, and can also damage your ability to be effective in relationships (Chapter 10,) and in your career (Chapter 11). Learning ways to regulate your feelings and to manage the intensity of your emotions is a critical functional skill you can use in all aspects of your life.

4. Interpersonal Effectiveness—Your effectiveness in relationships is very relevant as you work to heal the narcissism in your personality. As noted in Chapter 10, narcissism's hallmark is the inability to sustain meaningful, stable relationships. Many of the narcissistic patients I have worked with over the years originally came in for help to deal with relationship difficulties, whether with a spouse, children, co-workers, siblings, or parents. These problems keep them from feeling loved and accepted, and often contribute to their sense of isolation, rejection, and victimhood. This, in turn, only reinforces the narcissism in their personalities, which they use as their first defense against feeling defective and inadequate. To heal, you need to stop this vicious cycle. The skills DBT teaches in this area can help you understand basic principles of relationship building, so you can apply them in your everyday interactions. Because DBT includes group therapy, it gives you a forum for real-time interactions with other group members. This setting can provide genuine interpersonal feedback, as well as opportunities to practice and implement the relationship skills within the context of the group.

Interpersonal Therapy

The innovative psychoanalyst Harry Stack Sullivan first conceptualized interpersonal therapy in the mid-20th century. Gerald Klerman and

Myrna Weissman further developed it in the 1970s. This approach is a radical departure from classic psychoanalysis's focus on the unconscious. It emphasizes personality within the context of interpersonal relationships as a catalyst for emotional healing. Therapists with this orientation help patients understand which elements of their personality impede their ability to have healthy relationships. In therapy, patients gain the ability to achieve a healthier, more effective relationship with the therapist. The hope is that patients then can transfer the insights and skills they've learned in this positive interpersonal experience to their real-life relationships.

As mentioned, I was fortunate to have been trained by a protégé of Sullivan, Dr. Donald J. Kiesler, who ingrained in me the special role I can have as a therapist in giving my clients the invaluable gift of "interpersonal feedback." Therapy offers clients a rare opportunity to hear real, unfiltered feedback about how they have an impact on the people in their lives, and to develop the tools they need to make their relationships work. This therapy can help you understand your impact on other people and change things so that your relationships can improve. With interpersonal therapy, you can develop a better sense of yourself as a loveable, socially effective person.

Internal Family Systems Therapy

Internal Family Systems Therapy (IFS) is a particularly innovative and impactful approach to psychotherapy. It was first developed by Dr. Richard Schwartz, who recognized that trauma victims often have fragmented parts of their personality that conflict with each other. That can prevent someone from being the stable, consistent person he or she wants to present in relationships. This therapy involves identifying the different ego states within the individual's personality and doing actual quasi-family therapy sessions with the different internal states. The ultimate goal is for the person to develop what Dr. Schwartz called "self-leadership," the ability to manage these ego states, or parts, and to strengthen and facilitate the healthier, more adaptive ego states. This way they can take charge and become the dominant feature of the personality.

This can be a very powerful way to enable people who have narcissistic ego states that tend to kick in during periods of stress or conflict to gain control over these unhealthy parts of their personalities, and to allow the more adult, adaptive parts of their personality to take over. I have personally found that IFS therapy can be dramatically transformative by empowering people to develop the self-leadership that can help them to become the person they want to be in all of their relationships, even during periods of stress and conflict.

Narrative Therapy

First developed in the 1980s by Australian social worker Michael White and therapist David Epston of New Zealand, narrative therapy helps people write a new narrative about themselves and what they have experienced, so that their problems don't define their identity or sense of self. It is a way of externalizing problems, as opposed to personalizing them and making them the focus of the client's identity. As such, it is a sort of cognitive reframing of the patient's life experiences created collaboratively, with the therapist. The role of the therapist is to engage actively in assisting patients in rewriting their personal story in a more affirmative way that focuses on their assets and strengths, rather than deficits and pathology.

This type of therapy can help you if damaging life experiences shaped the way you feel about yourself or the way you define yourself as a person. Quite often, people—especially children, who tend to be self-oriented and to make everything about themselves—personalize abuse or neglect, and create a narrative that awful things happened to them because they are bad people and deserve to be mistreated. Their absorption of other people's problems makes it difficult for them to see the truth: that the abuse they suffered isn't their fault and isn't even really about them. It stems from the other person's bad behavior, caused by that person's problems and issues. As a result of not knowing this truth in a visceral way, some abuse victims develop narcissistic defenses against their underlying feelings of defectiveness and unworthiness. If through therapy you can develop a new narrative of what happened to you in your past, to depersonalize it through narrative therapy, then you no longer need the narcissistic defenses, and you can heal.

Trauma Therapy: Eye Movement Desensitization and Reprocessing

Because most people with narcissistic personalities or traits have experienced some sort of trauma or neglect, therapy that directly targets healing the traumas makes sense. Quite often, people's traumas shape their personalities, so if therapy can diminish or remove the trauma as an active force in your nervous system, the resulting personality features may recede, as well. Reducing or eliminating the source of a narcissistic personality feature makes it quite possible that, over time, and with the appropriate psychotherapeutic techniques, then the unhealthy personality features will fade.

I learned about Eye Movement Desensitization and Reprocessing (EMDR) from a long-time colleague, Laya Seghi, who introduced the concept to me during the early stages of its development, way back in 1994. She had just been trained in it, and as someone who is always at the cutting edge of things, she was completely enthusiastic about its potential impact and urged me to at least try it. At first, I thought that some strange technique that involved moving the eyes rapidly back and forth seemed like the snake oil of the 1990s, and I didn't give it much attention. However, after a while, and given Mrs. Seghi's further prodding, I agreed to allow her to practice the technique on Aaron, an unusually challenging patient, since I was having great difficulty breaking through his very strong narcissistic personality, and I hoped her strategy would help him.

CASE EXAMPLE 33: AARON

In Case Example 3, we spoke about Aaron, the attractive, successful 30-something businessman who was about to go through his third divorce. With his piercing blue eyes, charming personality, and financial prowess, he had no problem attracting women, most of whom were eager to marry him. However, once married, he showed an extreme intolerance for any negativity or criticism, which would invariably trigger rage, withering criticism, and complete emotional withdrawal. If his wife showed or expressed any negative feelings toward him, or in general, he would transform into a deeply narcissistic, insensitive person who saw her with antipathy and disgust. He had significant general problems with anger management, misogynistic tendencies, and unstable emotions, which made sustaining any relationship impossible.

Aaron grew up in a painfully traumatizing home, and he bore emotional scars that reflected his painful childhood. He had an abusive mother and a neglectful, passive father. The parents had a cold, distant relationship. Aaron's mother was abusive toward his father, who was passive-aggressive toward her. The more abusive she was, the more passive-aggressive he became, which only enraged her further. Growing up in this toxic environment damaged Aaron greatly,

However, after his first EMDR session, Aaron was significantly calmer, and instead of seeing his mother as this horrific witch whom he hated, he was able to begin to see her for who she really was—a very damaged Holocaust survivor who lost her entire family at a young age and had to manage on her own in a ghetto with no support. In the session, he reexperienced the hurt, the shame, and the rage associated with the memory of her slapping him after he came home with his bicycle broken—as a result of being hit by a car when he lost traction on an icy road. Instead of giving him the care and nurturing that he desperately needed at that moment for the pain and shock of being hit, she abused and shamed him for breaking the bicycle.

However, a relatively short period of time of EMDR, involving a lot of Mrs. Seghi waving her hands back and forth to elicit rapid eye movements (REM), greatly diminished the intensity of Aaron's emotions, and dimmed the clarity of this image when he tried to go back to the incident. As a result of the bilateral stimulation of his brain, he was also able to reactivate the processing mechanism of his left brain, and he was able to see his mother as a broken, damaged, traumatized woman who was incapable of dealing with such stress without becoming unglued.

His feelings of rage and disdain toward his mother gave way to profound feelings of empathy for what she went through as a child and a deeper understanding of her limitations as a mother. He was able to see her as a destroyed victim of horrific circumstances, who was damaged and was incapable of being the calm, nurturing mother he had longed for as a child. As a result of the EMDR session, he could desensitize some of the memories of abuse, and instead, focus on empathy toward his mother for all that she had gone through. He eventually healed from the trauma, as well as the narcissism, and was able to achieve a successful relationship, but only after a series of EMDR treatments.

So, how does EMDR really work? To appreciate its mechanism, consider how the brain normally processes everyday experience. The entry portal of the brain, through which our daily experiences enter, is the right brain, which is also the primary center of emotion (limbic system/amygdala) and memory (hippocampus). Your life experiences enter the nervous system through the right brain, which gets activated and then, in turn, activates the left brain. The two hemispheres then integrate, and collectively process the experience, which then dissipates into the nervous system. This prevents experiences from building up, and overloading the brain.

However, when we experience a trauma, instead of the right brain just becoming activated, it actually implodes, because of the intensity of the emotionality caused by the trauma. The rest of the nervous system then focuses on providing the neurological energy to maintain this intense reaction, leaving the left hemisphere de-energized and shut down. This causes the processing mechanism of the brain to go quiet, so no actual processing of the trauma occurs. As a result, the trauma stays active inside the nervous system, raw and unprocessed, with all of its original sights, sound, feelings, and smells fully intact. It stays stuck inside the hippocampus, the memory center of the brain, ready to be reactivated any time that you experience anything associated with the original trauma. This dynamic underlies the development of Post-Traumatic Stress Disorder, a psychiatric condition discussed in Chapter 6.

Quite often, when our conscious brain is "stuck" due to this dynamic of trauma, the unconscious brain kicks in, and tries to process the trauma through dreams. According to theories of dream activity, dreams are symbolic of unprocessed baggage stuck in the nervous system and represent disturbing unprocessed past experiences still harbored in the unconscious mind. When dream activity begins, the dreamer's eyes immediately begin to move rapidly from side to side, in an action called rapid eye movement, or REM. It happens to us all, especially as infants and young children.

We have known about REM for many decades, but science only recently offered a clearer understanding of what actually happens during REM. Briefly, three mechanisms (at least) seem to be operating when the eyes move back and forth rapidly. First, the action of rapid eye movement seems to stimulate the dormant left brain and, thus, reactivate the processing mechanism, allowing the traumatic material to move out of the nervous system. Second, chemicals released as a result of REM seem to disrupt the connection between the limbic system, the emotional center of the brain, and the traumatic memory. This results in a desensitization effect, in which the negative emotions—fear, anger, sadness—associated with the trauma lose some of the intensity they had before the REM.

In many cases, the emotions are completely gone, and the person no longer has an emotional connection to the traumatic memory. People who go through EMDR report that they can't access their intense feelings any longer, even when they deliberately revisit the trauma. Thirdly, the brain also releases chemicals that travel to the hippocampus, disrupting its connection with the images associated with the trauma, degrading the images and making them less accessible. Thus, REM explains how we often know that we've had a dream, but can't bring up the image or recall its contents.

Psychologist Dr. Francine Shapiro discovered in the late 1980s that when a person reexperiences or revisits a trauma, a spontaneous eye movement occurs that seems to create a fairly reliable desensitization effect. She wondered if therapists could use this knowledge about REM to help trauma victims. She experimented with eliciting REM in Vietnam War veterans, perhaps among the most traumatized people on Earth at the time, and found that—with a remarkable amount of reliability—it significantly diminished the intensity of their emotions and their attachment to their traumatic memories.

I found that truly remarkable, because I worked with Vietnam War vets during my 1986 internship at the VA Hospital in Richmond, Virginia, and found that most of them were hopelessly impervious to any treatment methods available at the time. It was quite disturbing to me, as a young therapist, to hear horrific stories such as a close hometown buddy being blown up right next to my patient when he was in Da Nang, and hearing how parts of his buddy's brain were splattered across his face. I felt profoundly sad and helpless that I had no ability to ease his trauma and intense pain or to affect him therapeutically in any significant way, other than to be an empathic listener, which really did nothing to heal his emotional wounds. If I'd had EMDR in my therapy toolbox at the time, the story would have been entirely different.

Dr. Shapiro then tried EMDR with other groups of trauma victims, and found that the effect was similar. In the next few years, she systematically researched this phenomenon and developed an eight-step protocol, now called Eye Movement Desensitization and Reprocessing. In the 26 years that I have been using EMDR, it has had a profound impact on my ability to help patients achieve a more complete and comprehensive healing from traumas.

When my colleague Laya Seghi came back from her training in EMDR, she was eager to share the experience with me, and tried to encourage me to take the training. I dismissed the suggestion out of hand. She persevered, however (fortunately for me), and asked me to come up with a patient with whom I was having the most difficulty. She offered to do an EMDR session with him, for his sake, as well as to give me an opportunity to see EMDR work firsthand. And that patient was Aaron, who is now leading a new life as a result of his work with EMDR.

For more information about EMDR or contacting a certified EMDR therapist, go to emdr.com for further assistance. An EMDR therapist can utilize this method in the context of therapy and weave it into the therapeutic process. Alternatively, you can use an EMDR practitioner along with your current therapist. EMDR can help you deal with your traumas while continuing to work on yourself in therapy. I have been working conjunctively as an EMDR practitioner with other therapists for many years. EMDR accelerates trauma victims' progress in the therapeutic process. This incredibly useful method can also facilitate the healing of personality issues associated with narcissism in a way that is very different than any other treatment method.

CHAPTER 16

The Power of Others:
Group Therapy ("Men's Group")

History

Historically, group psychotherapy has been an important addition to more traditional individual therapy, in that it provides those who participate a unique glimpse into the minds and hearts of others who may be experiencing similar challenges. Such groups can function as "support groups" in that members with similar issues have the opportunity to provide empathy and support to each other within the context of group therapy. People who have lost a significant other to recent death, or who may be struggling with a life-challenging illness, or who are dealing with the estrangement of a child, or who have a child who is mentally ill, all find a common ground in each other's experience. They also can find solace in the fact that they are not alone. The commonality of experience brings these people together, and this shared experience can give them strength and fill the void inside them.

Another type of group is called a "process group," because the focus is not so much on common experience, but rather on what is transpiring in the group itself. This type of group centers on the dynamics of the group process and what is happening in the moment, as opposed to what is happening in each member's life. This type of group can be very challenging, and often is not for the faint of heart. It allows individual members to express deeply felt feelings and, at the same time, give each other badly needed feedback, for instance, about the effect one member is having on the other members. This feedback often belies the core intent of the group: to foster growth and personal change as a result of the interpersonal interactions and feedback experienced in the group.

In 1995, as my practice began to include more couples in distress, it became apparent to me that quite a few of the men that I was seeing within these troubled marriages had been raised in disturbed, dysfunctional families. Their families of origin were almost uniformly centered around and affected by a narcissistic parent and, in some cases, two. These parents were self-centered, demanding, highly critical, and incapable of demonstrating the type of nurturing love a child requires to develop into a healthy adult who is capable of being effective in an intimate relationship.

For some of these men, nobody was home emotionally, since their parents were often so caught up in the drama of their relationships, unmet needs, frustrations and disappointments, that they had little left over to give their children. These men had learned as kids that to get their needs met, they had to fend for themselves. They were conditioned to focus on themselves and their unmet needs. Many of these men had developed the same characteristics as their parents and were causing their wives considerable pain and suffering. They were often insensitive to their wives' needs and solely focused on their own. They felt—and acted—as if their wives existed simply to meet their unique needs for respect, autonomy, sexual pleasure, and admiration. Many of these men were generally very difficult to live with and had anger management issues, stemming from their insecurities and hypersensitivity.

I realized that to maximize my ability to help these men truly heal, and to become better people, better partners and better parents, they needed more than their current individual psychotherapy and marital therapy. It became apparent that they needed a more dynamic, challenging experience that could happen only within the context of group therapy. So, I invited ten men whom I had been seeing at least a year to participate in an experience I innocuously referred to as a "Men's Group."

I intended to bring men together who were raised under similar circumstances, who were all struggling in their relationships, and who had narcissistic personalities, or at least traits of narcissism in their personalities.

By and large, they were insecure, needy, angry men who perceived themselves as victims of their wives' incessant demands and complaints. The truth was that, for the most part, they were the real problem.

Group Dynamics

At first, the men often fed off each other's negativity, and aligned with each other's sense of victimhood, often challenging me for confronting a group member's narcissistic thinking or behavior. They frequently projected anger onto me as an authority figure since they would identify in me, on an unconscious level, the narcissistic parent who was critical and judgmental of them. It took time for many of them to understand that my feedback was coming from a sincere desire to help them grow, rather than to put them down for my own self-aggrandizement, as was often the case with their narcissistic parents. Over time, many of the men became more receptive to feedback, and used it to facilitate their personal growth and development, as well as their ability to succeed in their relationships.

Often group members would call each other out for their narcissistic behavior, either in their personal lives or in the group. Sometimes the person would receive the feedback well and would grow from it. Other times, their reaction was anger, hurt, or defensiveness, since the member would feel that the group judged or misunderstood him. Narcissism sometimes had the effect of distorting their perceptions about what had happened, and they would project blame for their inappropriate behavior onto one another. The group often exposed and challenged revisionist thinking—when someone would alter the course of what happened to soften his own culpability. The group would confront the revisionist, often forcefully, for his attempts to distort history and defend himself when challenged.

Other dynamics began to emerge, as well. When the group called someone out on his behavior, sometimes that person would feel wounded and would become passive-aggressive—refusing to respond or share his feelings. Instead, he'd say he had nothing to say or didn't feel like sharing.

Others would stop coming for a while, and I would have to cajole them into attending the next meeting.

Another interesting dynamic developed when a few group members started to meet for dinner prior to the group meeting, and others would meet for a snack or drinks after each meeting. Personal relationships began to develop, leading to phone calls during the week to check in on each other, or to reach out when something distressing happened and a member sought advice or support. Over time, the group became a powerful resource for growth and change. It eventually evolved from an often-cantankerous bunch of angry, resentful victims to a group of insightful, self-aware, growth-oriented individuals, who were seeing positive results in their relationships. Change was clearly evident.

A different dynamic was evident, as well. The majority of the men in the group had developed sex addictions that they manifested in a variety of ways: repeated affairs, solicitation of prostitutes, pornography, compulsive masturbation and, in some cases, acting out sexually with other men. This became a subset within the group. The men who were dealing with such problems had the added challenge of having wives who were severely traumatized when they discovered these problems.

I encouraged these men to attend self-help groups such as Sexaholics Anonymous (SA), or Sex Addicts Anonymous (SAA), as a critical adjunct to our group. Since, as we discussed in Chapter 6, addictions are co-morbid factors often associated with narcissism, I wasn't surprised that a disproportionate number of our members were dealing with these kinds of addictions, especially since they often involve entitlement and self-justification. These men would rationalize that their actions were justified because they were the victims of their wives' anger and resentment.

These women uniformly were struggling deeply with a sense of betrayal and abandonment as a result of their husbands' often-outrageous behaviors. This vicious cycle frequently led to frustration and victimization among the men in the group, even though their behavior clearly brought on this pernicious cycle of resentment and acting out in the first place. In their minds, though, they were the ones who were the victims of their wives' anger and reactivity. They could not see the reality that they had victimized their wives in the first place.

Goals

Initially, my primary goals for the group were to promote a greater sense of awareness of the narcissism in their personalities and of how their particular traits affected the people in their lives. We shared a closely related goal of reaching a deeper understanding of how their upbringing contributed to their personality development. This often led to the painful epiphany that a parent or both parents were much more disturbed and damaging than they had ever realized.

Once the group established the broader goals of awareness, understanding, and insight, the members focused on more specific objectives. The men began to develop and practice communication skills, especially regarding relationships and conflict resolution, within the group. The next section describes some methods of communication in greater detail. These strategies were, and still are, the focus of the group.

Another very important group goal was to build members' self-esteem with positive reinforcement of the improvements they accomplished and demonstrated within the group. I find it very gratifying when a group member starts to display elements of humility and honesty, especially when he had previously acted in a bloated, deceptive way toward the group. Similarly, it is very gratifying when members report small successes in their behavior toward others and in their relationships. In these instances, I often ask the men if they see any difference in the way a specific member is talking or relating to the group. Invariably they report seeing a huge difference in how the person is functioning or speaking. A spontaneous outburst of applause often follows such positive feedback, and the look of pride and accomplishment on the face of the member being praised can be the highlight of my day.

Group members also want to define and clarify the goals of their important relationships. Over the years, many men often reevaluate the importance of their marriage, and the value of their wives, and recommit themselves to making their marriage work in ways that they were previously unable or unwilling to do. For them and their wives, the group is a gift that enabled them to develop the motivation and skills to make their relationships far more successful. On the other hand, the group gave other members the clarity to see that their spouses were unable to be healthy partners for them and their emotional recovery, and the strength to make the difficult decision to end their marriages. The members who decided to get divorced all ended up marrying women who were far more capable of partnering with them and making the relationship work. They are now quite happily married, as a result.

Success Stories

Over the 25 years that this group has been in existence, I estimate that approximately 100 men have been involved to one extent or another. Some came for one session, and a few continue to attend many years after their first meeting. Several stand out as success stories that highlight the effectiveness of the group as a catalyst for growth and change.

CASE EXAMPLE 34: JEFF

As a physician, Jeff had extensive contact with subordinates in his practice: office staff, nurses, interns, and residents. From the beginning of his marriage, he made sure the people in his world knew that he was "the boss." His extreme narcissism manifested in his constant barrage of orders and harsh criticism for people who did not live up to his often-unrealistic expectations. It also appeared in his rather frequent dalliances with young attractive staff members and nurses, as well as his salacious comments to other staff persons. His wife found out about his affairs and, instead of reacting harshly, she turned inward, shut down emotionally, and distanced herself from Jeff. He reacted as the victim, and then justified his behavior due to her lack of responsiveness and lack of respect for him and his hard work.

Group therapy was difficult for him at first. He came because he and his wife had come in for couples' therapy at the behest of their children who became aware of their problems. I had recommended the Men's Group as an important adjunct to therapy. At first, Jeff's arrogance and dismissive demeanor alienated the group, and made his integration as a member quite challenging. However, over time, he gradually began to respect the members for their forthright honesty and the high caliber of effort and integrity that they showed in the change process. He also, over time, earned their respect as they challenged him to reassess his perspectives about his wife and his marriage, as well as his attitude and behavior in the group.

Little by little, he became more humble and emotionally honest, and came to the realization that he did love and appreciate his wife. He also started to see that, in truth, he was the one who had alienated her, and not the other way around, as he had come to believe in his effort to project blame and distort the truth to justify his actions. He also started to develop healthy personal relationships with some members of the group, became active in Sexaholics Anonymous, and reengaged in his Catholic faith, which turned out to be a significant factor in his becoming a more humble, low-key person.

He left the group after being an active member for several years, so that he could devote more time to his wife and their activities in a church-sponsored couples group, as well as in doing community service together. When last I heard from Jeff, he was doing quite well. His marriage had healed to the extent that both he and his wife had decided to arrange for a recommitment ceremony to celebrate the new beginnings of a healthy, mutually satisfying marriage.

CASE EXAMPLE 35: NEIL

As a busy, successful attorney, Neil was under constant pressure to perform and to achieve increasingly high levels of financial success. He was a workaholic whose career was clearly his priority over his marriage and family. He expected his wife, Teri, to understand that being financially successful meant long hours at the office and frequent travel, leaving her to run the household and raise the children with virtually no support or interest on his part. These roles, and their respective expectations, were quite clear to Neil and unmovable. Although he was basically a well-meaning and ethical person, his rigid, dry way of dealing with people, including his staff, alienated nearly everyone.

His wife, who valued and needed the trappings of success, had no problem finding ways to spend money frivolously. At the same time, she deeply resented Neil for not being available to her, and she constantly displayed her anger and antipathy toward him. She subjected him to a relentless stream of criticism the moment he walked in the door. This forced him to avoid coming home, and he spent more and more hours at the office, throwing himself into his practice.

During marital therapy, it became clear that this was a Catch-22 situation in which both parties fed into the vicious cycle in their relationship. Although Neil was open to working on himself and, in fact, enjoyed the group, using it frequently for what he called "Narc Checks," Teri refused to participate in therapy at all. She would not take any responsibility for changing her attitude or behavior. Even though she knew her behavior was bringing out the worst in her husband, she chose not to work on herself, but instead continued to criticize and attack her husband relentlessly, seeing herself only as the victim.

Although Neil continued to work diligently on himself, and specifically his personality, he eventually grew apart from Teri, and, after a few years of being in the group, decided to get a divorce. He tried hard and succeeded in achieving a collaborative, "good" divorce, and he now has a more congenial relationship with Teri. His relationship with his children has improved, as a result of his new awareness about how he'd affected them previously. He has now met a woman with whom he has a mutually respectful and satisfying relationship, and he plans to marry her in the near future.

Dropouts

Over the years, quite a few men have tried to participate in the group, and for a variety of reasons, weren't able to make it work successfully for their individual needs. In the group's early years, before I fully understood the issue of severity of narcissism as a personality disorder (see Chapter 4), I encouraged any narcissistic male patient to join the group because of the powerful effect it had on its members and their relationships. However, along the way, I referred several men to the group whose narcissism was too severe for them to function there. They invariably convinced themselves that they were far too superior to participate in such a group of "losers." In fact, the members were often at a much higher level in terms of receptivity and intelligence, and actually had evolved quite a bit individually.

These highly narcissistic individuals often did not last beyond their first session, because they could not tolerate being in such an emotionally vulnerable situation. The idea of having one's weaknesses being exposed, or being identified publicly as a "patient," was far too threatening for them. Others participated for quite a while—in some cases, for years—and then left the group because of a perceived slight or insult, and convinced themselves that it was time to leave.

Others abruptly stopped coming for no apparent reason. When I reached out to them, they were often vague and said things like, "I wasn't getting as much out of it as I used to" or, "I'm just not feeling it anymore." When I tried to explore these feelings, I would often be met with flat resistance and little room for discussion. Some remained as individual therapy patients, and others dropped out of therapy altogether. Some would come back from time to time, but I never heard from or saw the others again.

CASE EXAMPLE 36: MITCH

Mitch was a surgeon who was deeply wounded by his narcissistic father, a man highly critical of all of his children, as well as his wife. Mitch spent the better part of his life trying to prove his worth by excelling in his specialized field and becoming a world-renowned expert in a particular type of innovative surgery. He was highly regarded as a surgeon and lecturer but, at home, he was a nightmare to live with. Arrogant, perfectionistic, and highly critical of his wife Sherry, he would often come home and bark orders at her and their children, focusing on what was wrong with their house, the children's performance in school, or what she or the children were wearing. He was a tall, handsome man, who was very preoccupied with physical appearance, and would often complain about minor imperfections in Sherry's face or body shape, with absolutely no clue or concern as to how damaging his criticisms were to her or to their relationship.

Mitch came in to therapy with his wife, who had been a patient of mine for several months. Sherry told him that she couldn't stay in the marriage unless things changed. I urged him to try the group, and he did so reluctantly, and had difficulty adjusting to the intensity and honesty of the group. Over time, he gradually acclimated somewhat to the dynamics of the group, but he still attended more sporadically than the rest of the group, due to his travel schedule. He reported different types of scheduling conflicts that seemed invariably to be more of a priority than attending the group.

After comments from group members, I challenged him about his irregular attendance. He went into a long diatribe about the great importance of his work, and how little I understood the extent to which he is world-renowned, and how unimportant and irrelevant the group really is in his life. When a group member with whom Mitch had an often-difficult relationship challenged his arrogance, Mitch erupted into a rage, verbally tore the other member apart, and abruptly flew out of the room. He never returned to the group, and soon after, dropped out of therapy altogether.

In Mitch's case, his ego was so fragile that he needed to be seen as extremely important, and he wanted the other men to know that he often had things to do that were more important than attending group. This mattered more to him than personal growth or a better family life. He also could not tolerate criticism to any real extent, and was unable to internalize much of what the men discussed because his narcissistic defenses made him minimize or degrade the value and validity of what was being said, as well as the people saying it.

Eventually, when their last child graduated high school, Sherry served him with divorce papers, and moved on with her life. Mitch was shocked and angry, blaming her for betraying him and for being disloyal. He eventually was diagnosed with Parkinson's disease, and had to retire early, trying to pick up the pieces of his shattered life alone—no career, no family, no friends gathered along the way. He stopped talking to his children, whom he felt abandoned him to side with his wife against him, even though it was his choice to stop communicating with them. Isolated, he spent most of his time alone, obsessively watching old clips of his lectures and old movies.

One Sunday morning, almost five years after I had last seen him, Mitch took out his gun and shot himself in the face. He died instantly.

Trip to Israel

In 2002, around five years after the group started, I came up with an idea for the men in the group that would have a transformational impact on all of them. I realized that a lot of what we discussed was abstract and not grounded in concrete reality, so I thought that a trip to Israel focused on extraordinary people who had met difficult challenges with resilience and grace would have a significant impact on them. In addition, the men had forged very close bonds by this point, since the group's membership had been about the same since its inception. They thought that such an intense experience would enhance the group's dynamic, and, at the same time, be potentially transformational and life-changing. I had no idea the extent to which the trip would turn out to be both.

Besides the usual destinations to such a land filled with historical sites and tourist attractions, we focused primarily on meeting people who had met adversity with a determination to turn their challenging, if not tragic, experiences into something meaningful that would have a positive impact on their world. Instead of taking on the roles of victims, which is what narcissists tend to do to elicit empathy and pity, these people turned around, and tried to turn tragedy into triumph. They were exactly the right antidote for the pathological narcissism that we were working on in group. They enabled the men to step outside of themselves and feel real empathy for people who had experienced such severe trauma. At the same time, the people that we met also served as role models for the way they faced adversity with dignity and strength, and not as victims, only focusing on how they could use their experiences to be a catalyst to do something meaningful for others.

We first met Dr. Leonard Epstein, whose son was killed in a terrorist attack several years earlier. Dr. Epstein was a retired physician who had established a name in the field of ophthalmology before moving to Israel in the 1980s. Instead of allowing his life to stop or to be destroyed by such a tragic loss, he decided to establish a string of outposts in the West Bank, an often dangerous area shared by Israelis and Palestinians alike, to provide hot soup, coffee, cold drinks, and snacks for soldiers who were stationed there and who put their lives in harm's way daily to protect the people who lived there.

At first, he had the means to set up the outposts, but he worried about how to get them serviced, given that he had set them up at the most dangerous, high-risk crossroads in the West Bank. However, instead of having difficulty getting people to work in these outposts, once word got out about what he was trying to accomplish, a long list of people who wanted to volunteer quickly emerged. He soon had a waiting list of people who wanted to travel to these lonely outposts to help these young boys feel that they were not alone by nurturing and taking care of them.

Dr. Epstein had turned his tragedy into something very meaningful that would make a difference in not only the lives of these young soldiers while they were undertaking such a difficult and dangerous task, but also in the lives of the volunteers who wanted to make a difference. Refusing to be a victim, he chose to be a positive force in his world.

We then met Abraham and Sarah, an extraordinary couple who had emigrated from Ethiopia several years earlier. Abraham, a slim man with intense eyes, was dressed in informal, contemporary clothes not unlike what his neighbors would wear, and his wife, Sarah, wore an elaborately decorated head scarf that was piled prominently on top of her head and a long flowing dress that obliquely reflected her native culture, but seemed unmistakably Israeli at the same time.

Their story was extremely compelling. They spoke about how they had to leave their small village in remote western Ethiopia, where they were part of a community of *Falashas,* or "strangers" in the local dialect, who lived as their ancestors did for centuries, practicing ancient Jewish rituals and customs that had been passed down for generations. As the political climate worsened in the late 1990s, it became clear that Israel had to orchestrate an effort to rescue the remaining Jews of Ethiopia. Israel devised Operation Magic Carpet, which brought thousands of Falashas to the Holy Land. However, they were able to help only when the people came to Addis Ababa, the capital. From there, El Al could whisk them to Israel to start their new lives.

In order to get to Addis Ababa, Abraham and Sarah had to walk by foot from their village, travelling for weeks with all of their remaining possessions on their backs, often encountering bands of marauding hoodlums, who would harass or attack them. They had to beg for water and food as they went from village to village, often in stifling heat, and at times, so fatigued and desperate that they started to lose hope. They kept going until they finally reached the capital and connected with the Israeli officials who were stealthily managing the rescue operations. They had never seen or even heard of an airplane, much less travelled in one, but there they were, in their traditional African garb, flying on the wings of an eagle to the far-off land of their forefathers, ready to begin their lives anew in the Jewish homeland.

Today, they live in the eastern outskirts of Jerusalem, in the thriving suburb of Maalei Adumin, where they sat with us in their small, but colorfully appointed living room. We listened to this modestly gentle couple talk about their ordeal and ultimate escape from the hell of a country that was imploding before their eyes. Instead of focusing on their hardships there and how they got here, or how difficult it was to live in a refugee camp, or, for that matter, how difficult it was to establish themselves as Black Jews in a predominantly white culture, they focused only on how grateful they were to be there, living openly and proudly as Jews. They were delighted to have the opportunity to work and raise their family in the Holy Land.

There was no hint of victimhood or resentment for what they had to go through to get to where they were—just gratitude and profound appreciation to G-d for helping bring them there. We sat there, spellbound by their deep spirituality and humility. We were profoundly touched by how they had moved forward with their lives with such incredible resilience. For many in the group, their story stood as a stark contrast to their focus on themselves as victims of their relatively tame challenges that they had built up in their minds as catastrophic.

Finally, we met Adam Lane, a man in his late 40s at the time who had a gently flowing greying beard and was robed in the traditional dress of the Hasidic Jew that he had become years earlier. A native of the small town of Danville, in south central Virginia, and an ordained Methodist minister, he and his German-born wife, a daughter of a Lutheran minister, were converts to Judaism. They had rejected the tenets of their families' faiths, and embraced Judaism in, of all places, Hamburg, Germany. He was studying for his PhD in Christian theology at the university there and, after many of his disturbing questions about some of the more basic tenets of Christianity went unanswered, he began to gravitate to Hamburg's chief Rabbi, with whom his journey toward Judaism began.

He described how the university faculty rejected him when they learned about his transformation. The university deprived him of receiving his doctorate though he was only three credits shy of completion. He discussed how difficult it was for his wife and children to adapt to life in Israel, at first, since they obviously were not born as Jews. They felt that they did not really belong in their former community or their new one either. He and his wife had eight children cramped in a small apartment in Jerusalem, and had great difficulty making ends meet, yet he and his incredibly dignified wife spoke of their challenges with profound faith and gratitude for the choices that they made, despite the hardships they had encountered. Their story moved the men in their group, who were astounded by the couple's courage and indomitable strength, as well as their determination to follow their deep convictions, regardless of the challenges that undoubtedly lay ahead.

In addition to meeting these incredible people, the group had several experiences that affected them greatly. Several stand out in my mind. One involved Alan, a member of the group, who was a bit of an outlier, because his narcissism was interlaced with a relatively rare clinical disorder called Schizoid Personality Disorder. People with this disorder have little or no need for relationships or, for that matter, to be with people at all, and often have great difficulty interacting in groups. Alan had been a part of the group for quite some time at that point, but did not integrate into the group bonding experience as well as the other members. On the trip, he would often drift off alone or fall behind, so we often had to find him to get him to catch up with the group.

At one point, we were on an outing, and our tour guide had brought a bag of sandwiches, half of which were egg salad, and the other half tuna salad. It quickly became apparent that most of the men weren't interested in the egg salad sandwiches, so there was a bit of a mad grab for the tuna sandwiches. Unfortunately, some of the guys who were hoping for the tuna were left with the egg salad, but it also became apparent that the numbers didn't add up. There should have been five tuna sandwiches, but instead there were only four. We then realized that someone must have taken two tuna sandwiches for himself, leaving the additional egg salad sandwich for some poor, unsuspecting soul.

I had noticed that Alan had been busy earlier, hurriedly downing a sandwich, and he was now eating another one with the rest of the guys. It dawned on me that he was, indeed, the culprit of the "great tuna fish heist." It was a rather heavy choice point for me, since I didn't want to humiliate Alan, but at the same time, I couldn't let such an outrageously selfish move go unaddressed.

So, I quietly took him aside, told him what I suspected had occurred. After he sheepishly confirmed that my hunch was correct, I asked him what he felt was the right thing to do. He offered to share with the group what he had done, which he did, and then apologized for his selfishness. Years later, he told me that the famous tuna fish incident had made a profound impact on him, because it took such a clear, concrete example to help him realize how selfish he can be. Afterward, he redoubled his efforts to be generous and other-centered. This ultimately led him to get married—for the first time—at the age of 52.

For years after the trip, the men in the group would reflect back on these experiences, and take in and internalize the lessons that they had learned to assist them in their journey toward healing. These lessons improved their ability to be effective in their relationships. They also recalled the extraordinary people that they had met to help inspire their own resilience and to strengthen their attempts to conquer their narcissism and victimhood. They ultimately used their experiences on this trip to replace their narcissistic personalities with humility and found the courage to transform themselves into the mature, caring people that they knew that they could become.

These experiences underscore the powerful impact of the group therapy dynamic, without which these men would never have achieved what they accomplished in terms of self-awareness, the ability to bond, and personal growth. This Men's Group demonstrated what researchers have suggested for decades: A group therapy experience can elicit profound changes in people who participate actively in the process. In combination with individual (and marital therapy, when relevant), it can have a far deeper impact on the process of healing and recovery from narcissism than individual therapy alone.

CHAPTER 17

Improving Relations: Empathy and Relationship Skills Training

Empathy Training: The MORE Method

Having a narcissistic personality often severely affects the ability to have empathy for the plight of another person. Empathy requires being able to step outside of yourself and to feel what another person is feeling; that ability is significantly impaired in narcissistic people. Empathy also requires being aware that other people have their own pain, but narcissistic people are so preoccupied with their pain that they lack the ability to even be aware that their behavior is hurting someone else.

Years ago, when I started to focus my work on people with narcissistic personalities, I realized that, at some elemental level, this condition involves a skills deficit. The skills deal with the ability to communicate and respond effectively when triggered and, perhaps more broadly, to relate to people in an effective way that promotes healthy relationships. I ran a generic analysis of the factors that go into relating effectively to another person, and came up with four broad factors that I find important to focus on in therapy. The acronym MORE captures the four steps in a way that helps you to remember the basic elements of being empathetic:

1. Mindfulness—This relates to the ability to be mindfully aware of what you are doing to have an impact on another person. More broadly, it is important to be aware of what is going on at a macro level, such as the fact that you want the relationship to work. Also, the person you're affecting has his or her own issues and needs that you must consider, instead of dwelling only on your own needs.

2. <u>O</u>ther-centered—Try hard to push yourself out of your self-centered focus. This involves shifting your point of reference away from yourself and toward the other person as the focus of your attention. Force yourself to see things from the other person's perspective. Asking yourself questions such as, "What is he/she thinking, feeling, needing right now," can help you to be more other-centered and to respond with care and nurturing, not anger, resentment, or neediness.

3. <u>R</u>eframe—Instead of judging, criticizing, or devaluing other people or their behavior, try to reframe what happened from a place of empathy and understanding. Reframing involves the ability to turn things around in your mind away from a negative framework and toward seeing things from the other person's perspective in a more positive, forgiving way.

4. <u>E</u>mpathy—If you have empathy, you can put yourself in someone else's shoes, understand what they are experiencing, and feel their pain. Feeling badly for what another person has gone through can help you put their reactions in perspective, even if you'd otherwise feel victimized by their behavior. It will help you to prevent yourself from feeling as if you are the victim. This is especially important and challenging, if you provoked the reaction, and the other person's behavior is actually a response to what you did to cause him or her hurt or damage. Empathy can soothe your soul, give you a more realistic take on what is truly happening, and help you respond with awareness and understanding, not harsh judgment or rage.

The MORE method requires you to follow and implement the first three steps effectively so you can arrive at the fourth step, empathy. In other words, to be truly empathetic and to respond effectively under fire, you first have to take a step back, wait a minute, and think of the big picture, both in terms of what you really want to accomplish in a particular situation, and in terms of understanding other people—who they are and what they have gone through with you or in their life in general.

Then, push yourself out of your view of a situation. Move away from your frame of reference and force yourself to see things from the other person's perspective. Try, as hard as it may be, to see things from his or her vantage point. Next, reframe what you are experiencing away from seeing the other person as the villain with you as the victim. Shift things in your mind to frame them differently, to see things more neutrally or positively, without judgment or anger influencing your perception.

Then, and only then, can you truly achieve true empathy and use it to respond effectively when you have been provoked by another person's angry reactions or criticism.

When I work with people who are struggling with narcissism, I teach the MORE method fairly early on in therapy, and invoke the phrase MORE when a person is reacting narcissistically. This prompts the person to stop how they are reacting, and to try to take a step back, and think—to be aware and mindful of what is happening. Mindfulness is a left-brain activity that involves processing and thinking more objectively. Just thinking in a mindful way can activate the more logical left brain and shut down the emotional reactivity of the right brain's limbic system. This can calm you down and help you become more rational in your thinking.

Just prompting yourself to use MORE can help position yourself to think calmly and work things through in your mind. Hopefully, this will lead you down the path of empathy and result in more positive, effective interactions with other people.

Conflict Resolution Training: The RVRR Method

Conflict, a common issue in most relationships, emerges when people have arguments, disagreements, or conflicting agendas or needs. It is not only common, it is normal for people, especially couples, to have conflict in their relationships. Many will claim that it is actually healthy to have conflict and to have the skills that are necessary to resolve conflicts effectively. Many couples actually find that their relationship improves when they face a conflict and are able to resolve it collaboratively, together.

Early in my career, I realized that conflict resolution is a critical skill that people must have in order to succeed in any relationship. I saw that it would be vital for me to be able to help patients resolve conflicts in their lives. In working with people with narcissism, I have also realized, unfortunately, that they are far more likely to have difficulty with conflict, because of their heightened sensitivities and their inability to see things from the perspective of another person. Far too often, their approach is, "my way or the highway." Their inability to compromise and their propensity to argue makes it uniquely difficult for them to handle interpersonal conflict effectively.

In the early 1990s, I developed a systematic, structured method of conflict resolution that reflected what I thought were the critical elements that must be addressed to resolve any conflict. The four steps of RVRR (pronounced "River") are:

1. Reflect—Repeat or paraphrase what the person initially says when you begin an interaction that could trigger a potential conflict. Start with a phrase such as, "So, what I am hearing you say is...", or "So, what I think you are trying to say is...", which is basically a retelling of what is being heard with no additional commentary—just what you heard. This is very important in any conflict resolution effort because it tells the other person that he or she is being heard. In this case, that the other person took the time, and made the effort to listen carefully to what was said. This sets the tone of the discussion to allow it to remain respectful and collaborative, rather than to devolve into an argument. It also encourages the person you are listening to make more of an effort to listen to you, and to reflect back what you are saying.

2. Validate—Once you reflect what you heard from the other person, the next step is to validate what he or she said to you. That can be a simple, "I hear you," or "I hear what you are saying." Other examples of validation might be, "I can understand that," or "If I were you, I would feel the same way." This communicates to the other people that you heard what they said, and you can understand how they feel as well. This sets the stage for a mutually respectful dialogue that will inevitably lead the

other person to be more receptive to hearing what you are saying and to validate your feelings, as well.

3. <u>Respond</u>—Once you reflect back to other people what you heard them say, and then validate them and their message, you will be in a much better position to respond effectively because you have established a framework of collaboration and cooperation. You have set the stage for the other person also to be more receptive to hearing you. However, when you respond, remember three general tips for effective communication that you can easily apply to conflict resolution:

➤ Use "I" statements and avoid using the word "you"—So, instead of saying, "You are really a nightmare to work with," say "I am finding it difficult to work like this."

➤ Use "feeling" statements instead of judging the other person—So, instead of saying, "You were really awful when you said that," say "I felt hurt when you said that."

➤ Use passive statements, rather than active statements—So, instead of saying, "You hurt me," try "I was hurt by that."

Responding appropriately and effectively when you are being confronted is an important first step in the RVRR process. It can help turn an interaction away from being combative and confrontational, and toward being collaborative and mutually respectful.

4. <u>Resolve</u>—Once you have reflected, validated, and responded, you are finally at the point of resolution. Now, someone should initiate the comment, "So, how do we resolve this?" This enables you to steer the encounter into being a more collaborative discussion about possible solutions to the conflict, rather than listing all the reasons you are right, and sparking an endless continuation of the arguments surrounding the conflict. Over several decades of working with difficult personalities, I have found four ways of potentially reaching some sort of resolution to a conflict. I've listed them in order of preference, starting with the most preferable:

➤ **Give in**—When one person decides to give in and does so graciously, that is by far the most effective way of resolving a conflict. It also builds an environment of trust and a spirit of cooperation that will invariably strengthen the relationship and make it more likely for the other person to be more flexible and open to giving in the next time there is a conflict.

➤ **Look for a compromise**—Brainstorming ideas for a compromise can be a fruitful way of finding solutions to a conflict. It enables both parties to work together to find common ground, instead of digging in their heels and holding their own ground. If the environment is safe, and the participants respect each other and carefully consider any idea for a potential compromise, instead of immediately shooting it down, the atmosphere of cooperation can develop and deepen. Then, the participants are more likely to identify potential solutions and agree to them in a spirit of cooperation.

➤ **Defer to another time**—Sometimes when the disagreement becomes more heated, and the atmosphere for cooperation and finding solutions starts to deteriorate, it is often best to take a break and reschedule a further discussion. Find a time when both parties are better rested, thinking more clearly, and focused on the goal of resolution, rather than on being right or winning the argument. This keeps the conflict from devolving into an out-and-out fight and moves it off the table long enough to allow both parties to recenter themselves. Then they can come back in more of a spirit of collaboration, so they can focus on finding a solution that can work for everyone involved.

➤ **Defer to another person**—When the conflict is beyond a resolution, it is best to defer to a person both of you trust. This could be a close friend, your therapist, a clergy person, or another neutral party. Look for someone who can be an effective arbiter.

The RVRR method can help you, not only in terms of resolving conflict, but also in becoming a more other-centered person and being more effective in all of your relationships.

Adventure in Intimacy: From the Workshops of Hedy Schleifer

One of the challenges of people who struggle with narcissism is the inability to be emotionally intimate, in a real sense, with a partner. Intimacy requires a number of personal traits, all of which are necessary to make a close, committed relationship work:

➤ **Emotional openness**—The ability to get in touch with and be open and honest about how you feel.

➤ **Emotional expressiveness**—The ability to verbalize comfortably what you are feeling.

➤ **Vulnerability**—Being able to acknowledge your weaknesses, fears, or needs.

➤ **Healthy conflict resolution skills**—Being able to resolve conflicts in a collaborative and mutually respectful manner that can lead to closeness and connection.

➤ **Authenticity**—The ability to be honest and transparent in your interactions.

➤ **Connectability**—The ability to connect in a meaningful way that brings a sense of closeness and intimacy.

People with narcissistic traits often lack these abilities, and such deficits can lead to relationship difficulties and failures. Working on developing these abilities and skills can be very helpful in improving the quality of relationships and can enable the experience of true intimacy with a significant other.

An extraordinarily gifted therapist, Hedy Schleifer, a colleague who lived for many years in Miami Beach, gives an immensely effective workshop called Adventure in Intimacy. She brings couples in from around the world to experience an intense weekend exploring the reasons why intimacy is not a part of their relationship and learning how to bring it back. She focuses on building communication skills and providing experiences that can foster deeper connections. The workshop creates a safe place within which couples can allow themselves to be more emotionally open and expressive and to be vulnerable and authentic with each other in ways that they were never able to.

I have sent many couples to this workshop, and most felt that it was transformative, and that it dramatically changed the dynamic of their relationships. In her deeply authentic and warm manner, Hedy gently moves couples toward each other to promote a sense of intimacy and bonding that many have never experienced. Even in cases where trauma derailed the relationship, they were able to regain the trust and closeness they once shared.

Some patients with narcissistic personalities who attend these workshops find it challenging at first, because the open communication and vulnerability can be quite uncomfortable and threatening. However, Hedy's incredible sincerity and genuineness usually disarms them, and she eventually assists them in developing these critical relationship skills and in feeling better about themselves as partners or spouses.

While Hedy and Yumi no longer offer the Adventure in Intimacy workshop, Hedy continues to share these same principles in her private work with couples.

Imago Therapy—Getting the Love You Want: Harville Hendrix

The concept of Imago Relationship Therapy is based on the theory that we all have an internalized image inside of us that represents the unfinished business and "baggage" associated with our opposite-sex parent, or the parent with whom we had the most difficulty while growing up. The theory suggests that we gravitate toward people who represent that imago, in an effort to repair whatever was wrong with that earlier relationship. Unfortunately, when people end up with partners who are associated with their parental wounds, those traits are very likely to trigger them, and they usually end up with conflict as old wounds are reawakened.

The Getting the Love You Want workshop opens the door to growth and change by helping you understand the dynamics of your past experiences and how they affect the dynamics of your partnership. You and your partner learn the principles, processes, tools, and skills that are needed for mindful, conscious relationship. Imago theory suggests that humans possess a natural impulse for self-repair, self-completion, and loving connection. Cooperating with these natural impulses means opening up to unforgettable lessons about life, love, and healing. This workshop can promote new awareness and skill development that can literally transform your relationship, and allow you to achieve greater healing, communication, and life satisfaction.

If you are someone with narcissistic personality traits, this workshop and other general approaches to couples therapy can give you valuable insight and feedback about how your background has affected you and your ability to sustain a relationship. More importantly, it can give you important tools to counteract these effects and to turn your relationship around and make it more meaningful and fulfilling.

For Family Members: Effective Strategies for Successfully Dealing with a Narcissist

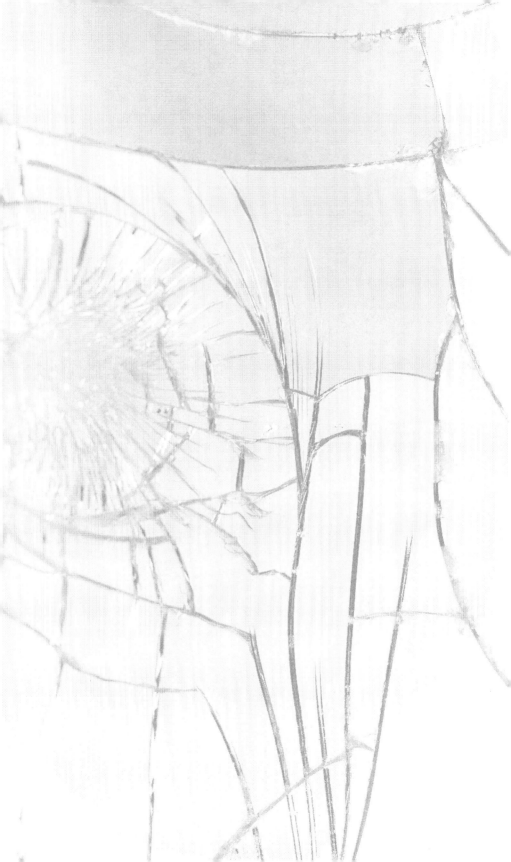

CHAPTER 18

Holding on to the Whole Picture:
Mindful Awareness

A Note to the Reader

If you have a narcissistic personality, you need to understand that dealing with a narcissistic partner, spouse, parent, sibling, child, or boss can be a debilitating experience. If you can allow me to take a break from talking to you now, and shift the focus to the people in your life, you can also gain a lot of insight into their struggles and, perhaps, help them to work with you more effectively and to help themselves.

Remember, they are still here because they love you, and they want to make things work.

Life with a Narcissist

Trying to establish a relationship with someone who has difficulty making a relationship work can be stressful and demoralizing. It takes a toll on your life and threatens your self-image, confidence, sense of self, and general level of energy. If you are not careful and effective, it can take over your life, and cause serious emotional and physical effects. It is important for you to develop the necessary tools and strategies to be able to manage this challenge. This is true both in terms of being effective in dealing with the person, and also in being able to develop the self-care strategies to help you stay emotionally afloat.

This section provides you with ideas and helpful recommendations so you can be more successful in your relationship, and more effective in taking care of yourself, which may be the most important thing of all.

Definition of Mindfulness

There isn't really one, singular way of defining "mindfulness." It basically means being attuned to what you and, perhaps more importantly, the people in your world, are feeling, thinking, wanting, or needing. According to the originator of Mindfulness-Based Stress Reduction, Jon Kabat-Zinn, mindfulness is an approach to life based on understanding that "the present is the only time that any of us have to be alive—to know anything—to perceive—to learn—to act—to change."

Practicing mindfulness means developing the ability to pay deliberate attention to your internal and external experiences from moment to moment in an open, curious way. Relating compassionately to life in this way and learning to direct (and redirect) your attention toward the present moment allows for greater access to your own powerful resources for intuition, insight, creativity, and healing.

In the practice of mindfulness, your mind observes thoughts and feelings as events, without over-identifying with them and without reacting to them in an automatic, habitual way. This state of self-observation introduces a "space" between your perceptions and responses. In this way, practicing mindfulness helps you respond reflectively to situations instead of reacting to them reflexively based on conditioned habits or ingrained behavioral patterns. By practicing mindfulness, you can shift your relationship to yourself and your life experiences in a way that allows for greater acceptance and compassion and, in doing so, you can dramatically improve the quality of your life and your relationships.

When you are dealing with a narcissistic person, practicing mindfulness can help you manage your emotions and behavior by allowing you to distance yourself from patterns of neural pathways that have persistently led you to be highly reactive to the anger, manipulation, and distortion that often characterize narcissistic behavior. Being mindful of what is happening at any given moment, both internally within yourself and in the dynamic between you and the other person, can help you give yourself the space to process what you are experiencing and to respond, instead of react.

Practicing mindfulness by allowing yourself to breathe, think, and process before responding to toxic behavior can reduce the extent to which that behavior triggers you to react in a way that will only fuel the fire of the narcissist's rage and victimhood. Instead, mindfulness can enable you to respond in a way that maintains your composure and dignity while trying to keep the emotional heat in the space between you and the narcissist in your life to a minimum.

Keeping a Sense of Perspective

The way to keep a healthy perspective when dealing with a loved one (or boss) who is narcissistic is closely related to the concept of mindful awareness. It can help you maintain perspective by keeping calm and reminding yourself that you want to remain in control and not allow yourself to be triggered by the narcissist's behavior. Remembering where the narcissist came from, how he or she got this way, why you want to make the relationship work, and how to take the high road, will help you maintain your perspective when you are dealing with a difficult person.

For me, personally, having a sense of perspective also means being effective, and I try to keep that concept in mind in dealing with all the relationships in my life, especially with patients and those closest to me. This involves dealing with people in a manner that lets me achieve my goals in my interactions, while being mindful of the other person's thoughts, feelings, and needs. I actually succeed, at times, in being effective, although perhaps not as consistently as I would like, because it can be difficult to maintain your composure under fire from a degrading, manipulative narcissist.

Relating to a narcissist can be especially difficult if you were raised in a narcissistic home or had a previous relationship with a narcissist. The behavior you are experiencing with a narcissist now is triggering old neural pathways that connect to those earlier traumatic experiences. Being aware of the baggage that you carry into today's relationship, and how this person is affecting you within the context of your past toxic relationships, is also a way of keeping a sense of perspective. Being mindfully aware of what is inside of you can help you stave off being triggered.

Using the MORE Method and RVRR

Developing specific relationship and communication skills can be very effective in improving your relationships, but it's never more important than when you are dealing with someone who has a narcissistic personality. The MORE (mindfulness, other-centered, reframe, empathy) method, as noted in Chapter 17, can be an invaluable tool in developing a higher level of effectiveness in dealing with your partner.

1. Mindfulness—Being mindful forces you to look at the bigger picture, which is that he or she is damaged and unhealthy. It also requires you to be in control and strategic in the way that you respond, rather than just letting yourself be triggered and then emotionally exploding.

2. Other-centered—Being other-centered is equally critical, so you don't fall into the victim trap by focusing only on your pain and how angry you are as a result of the behavior to which you are being subjected. Focusing on the other person's perspective and trying to understand what he or she is experiencing can enable you to stay calm and be, once again, more effective in dealing with the situation.

3. Reframe—Reframing what you hear or experience in a more positive way can help avoid being triggered and reactive. Instead of focusing on the most negative aspects of the person's behavior, try to reframe the experience within the context of something that would help you neutralize your feelings, so you feel less angry or judgmental.

4. <u>Empathy</u>—Having empathy allows you to understand what the other person has experienced in his or her life and to have compassion for what he or she went through. This enables you to put the other person's behavior in perspective and to avoid focusing on yourself as a victim.

Finally, remember that narcissists behave as they do for a reason, and that the abuse or neglect that they suffered is why they act this way. If you can, try to be empathetic toward them and see beyond their behavior. Then, you will be more likely to keep your cool and succeed in the goal of maintaining your composure and dignity.

I often ask narcissists' partners to have a mental image in their mind of their partner as a child being mistreated or neglected and to remember what it must have been like to have had that painful experience when they were so young. Maintaining one's empathy when facing fire is perhaps the best way to respond as you'd ideally like to in handling a situation, as opposed to allowing yourself to be triggered and lose control of your emotions and behavior, which inevitably only makes things worse.

CASE EXAMPLE 37: LEANNE

Leanne was a bright, intuitive, and sensitive mother of two young girls. In her mid-30s, she discovered that her husband, Tom, her childhood sweetheart in their small hometown in Wisconsin, had not only been having a lengthy sexual relationship with a saleswoman in his auto dealership, but also had an extensive history of seeking prostitutes, massage parlors, and strip joints during the course of most of their marriage. Finding out about his severe sexual addiction was a total shock to her, because, otherwise, she saw him as basically a decent man who worked hard to support his family, even though he could be rough at times. She had no idea that his long hours away from home at night were not about being at work, but were more of a pretext as a way to feed his need for a multitude of sexual pursuits.

She eventually learned that Tom's father had been an alcoholic who was physically abusive toward him and his brother. He would often not come home at night, leaving his mother petrified and furious. Tom's mother had been unable to focus on her children's needs, because she was preoccupied with her husband's misdeeds. She seldom paid attention to Tom's fears and the emotions he felt about his father. He was a victim of his father's abuse and his mother's emotional neglect. He learned early in life that sexual thrills numbed the pain he held inside at a deeper level. This quest evolved into a full-force sexual addiction.

Leanne's sudden realization that what she had thought was a nearly perfect life was really a façade, and that the man that she had thought was her best friend and someone that she could absolutely trust, was actually a sociopathic fraud, shook her to her core, and affected her in a deeply traumatic way. Leanne had grown up in a home where her narcissistic father ruled the roost, and thoroughly dominated her mother, her sisters, and her. She had developed a high sensitivity to dishonest behavior as a result of finding out about her father's infidelity and shady business dealings. She thought that, at least, she had an honest husband, even though he could be, at times, insensitive and controlling. To find out the truth about what had been going on all those years triggered her deeply, because it took her back to the dynamics of her family of origin, which she had previously been able to compartmentalize and lock in a drawer, never to be dealt with in her present life.

As a result, Leanne's reactions were extreme and, when triggered, she would sometimes verbally and physically abuse Tom. She would become emotionally dysregulated and unable to control her feelings when Tom's behaviors reactivated those deep wounds and brought them to the surface. As a result of what he perceived as his wife's crazy, abusive behavior, Tom focused only on being a victim as opposed to focusing on his actions, which caused her reaction in the first place.

They came in for treatment on the verge of a separation, both feeling very wounded and hopeless about the survival of their marriage. We pursued many months of therapy for both Leanne and Tom. Leanne's case called for intense EMDR, as well as trauma-focused cognitive therapy, emotional body work, and ego state therapy (more on that to come). She became more stable, and more able to express her feelings calmly toward Tom when his behavior triggered her rage.

Through learning and applying the MORE and RVRR methods, she became much more effective in responding to Tom, rather than reacting to him. This reduced the defensiveness and victimizing that he normally would resort to when he felt attacked. Most importantly, she was able to develop true empathy for her husband, and what he went through as a child, which softened her considerably, and helped him with his healing process. Eventually, they were able to regain some stability in their relationship, and Leanne's greater effectiveness in dealing with Tom helped him to work harder on his narcissism and addiction in his own therapy, with a priority on keeping it out of their relationship.

CHAPTER 19

Becoming an Effective Partner:
Strategic Thinking

Becoming a Strategic Thinker

Whenever we face a challenge in our lives, we often find the need to stop and think about what we need to do to deal with the challenge or to resolve the problem. We typically think about what strategies or approaches to the problem that are available to us, consider the pros and cons of each option, and then logically choose which will be the most effective choice—and then we calmly and deliberately implement it.

That is usually what happens with us when we are challenged, right? Wrong. Definitely not. As emotional beings, we often do the opposite of that. We react emotionally and shoot from the hip, because we have been emotionally triggered and, therefore, our ability to think logically is impaired.

When you are in a relationship with someone with a narcissistic personality, it is often the case that their behavior triggers you. You feel hurt, insulted, angry, even enraged by what they have said or done. Then, of course you react right back at them—hurling insults, criticizing, and otherwise expressing your pain in any way possible, other than, of course, the ways that could be most effective in accomplishing the goal of getting him or her to understand how they hurt you and how damaging their behavior is to you and the relationship.

However, if you go back to the concept of mindfulness, and you stop and process what is happening and what you want to accomplish, without allowing yourself to indulge in the usual negative emotional reactions, you can then begin to *think* through, rather than *feel*, what possible options are available to you. Once you have done that, then you can strategize a way to accomplish whatever goal you may have—to get your partner to understand how you feel, and to find a way to resolve the conflict between the two of you.

Definition of Strategic Thinking

Generally speaking, strategizing can be defined as the ability to think through ways to get something accomplished or to devise a series of steps that are necessary to achieve your goals. When you utilize strategic thinking, you are concentrating on the end goal, and how to get there, as opposed to getting caught up with the emotions of the moment after being triggered.

When dealing with a narcissistic spouse, it is extremely important to not allow your emotions to "hijack" you, but, rather, to keep your emotions in check, and to think through how you wish to handle him or her in a way that is most effective. Most often, being strategic and thinking through your various options in handling the situation will be the best way to accomplish your goals. These include communicating what you feel in a controlled and respectful manner, not losing your personal dignity by reacting harshly, and keeping the relationship intact by avoiding strong emotional reactions and insulting comments which are likely only to exacerbate the narcissism.

Being strategic also involves making a conscious choice to be your best, to take the high road, and to use your brain as a resource to come up with effective responses and solutions to a problem, rather than giving in to your emotions. It also requires you to consciously not allow old neural pathways to take over your actions and to send you back to old triggers and emotional reactions associated with this type of behavior from people in your past. Rather, it forces you to stay in the moment, use your thought processes to work your way through the various options you may have, and choose the one that will be the most likely to succeed in neutralizing the situation and achieving a more positive outcome.

Responding Versus Reacting

Strategic thinking is closely related to the concept of being responsive, as opposed to reactive. Being responsive is a cognitive process that involves considering your options and responding to your partner in a way that will be most effective in addressing his or her needs, feelings, or opinions. As opposed to being reactive, which is really nothing but an emotional reflex, responding is a thought-out way of handling a situation. It is also other-centered, because it requires you to think about your partner and what would be best for him or her. This stands in contrast to the self-centeredness of reactivity, which is all about you and why you are entitled to be upset. When you allow yourself to be reactive, you are actually, in a way, being narcissistic.

Responding to your partner, instead of reacting, will more probably result in an outcome that comes closer to achieving what you would like to accomplish in the situation. It is also more likely to elicit a more positive response from your partner and also to build the relationship up in a positive way. Responding, rather than reacting, is also less likely to elicit a narcissistic response from your partner, and over time, can actually diminish the narcissism that you experience from him or her in general.

Left Versus Right Brain

As we discussed previously, the brain is separated into two hemispheres, the left and the right. Generally speaking, the left brain is where we process our experiences, and where logic and reason is paramount. It's the rational, cognitive, intellectual part of our brain.

The right brain, on the other hand, is where the emotional part of the brain lies, which is also called the limbic system. The heart of the limbic system is an almond-shaped body called the amygdala, which fires off when we get emotionally triggered. This process is often called the "amygdala hijack," the reaction that happens when we get flooded by our emotions and can't objectively or calmly process what we are experiencing.

The right brain is also where the memory center of the brain, the hippocampus, is dominant. This is where our memories are stored, and they also become activated when we are triggered. The hippocampus is where our "baggage," our traumatic or damaging experiences, lie in the nervous system, raw, unprocessed, and ready to jump out and invade our consciousness when we are triggered by a situation that is similar to or associated with our baggage. So, when you experience with your partner the same type of critical, dismissive, or humiliating behavior that you endured as a child from a parent, sibling, or classmate, you will react not only to the present situation with your partner, but you also will experience the rage, hurt, or fear of those old experiences that are stored in your hippocampus.

The goal in managing yourself and your relationship with someone with a narcissistic personality is to stay in the left brain, and not to allow your right brain to take over and hijack you. Staying in the left brain will more likely lead you to respond, rather than react. It also enables you to activate your brain's processing mechanism, which allows you to work through in your mind what is actually happening in the moment, and to assess what are your available options, and which you think will be most effective in dealing with your partner. It also will help you to stay calm and emotionally in control, and less likely to be emotionally hijacked.

My experience in terms of the best way to achieve the goal of staying in the left brain is through the bilateral stimulation associated with EMDR. This bilateral stimulation actually activates the left brain and, in turn, deactivates and calms the right brain. Neuropsychiatric research has actually shown the activation of the left brain, and the relative lowering of activation in the right brain, as a result of EMDR's bilateral stimulation of the brain. As discussed previously in the section on EMDR, it also more broadly desensitizes the nervous system, especially with regard to the stimulus that is triggering you, and it facilitates your processing of the event, thus enabling you to respond to it in a better way, instead of reacting to it.

When I work with patients who have baggage that gets triggered in interpersonal conflicts, I teach them self-EMDR, which is basically finding the best mechanism through which a particular individual can achieve bilateral stimulation of the brain. For some, finding two points in the corners of the visual field in front of them, and shifting visually back and forth between these two points, is the best way to achieve bilateral stimulation. For others, tapping on their thighs, alternating left and right, may be most effective in achieving bilateral stimulation. Still others prefer auditory bilateral sounds that can be delivered through special headphones offered by various companies that sell EMDR equipment online.

Regardless of your preferred method of achieving bilateral stimulation, the key is to be aware that you have been emotionally triggered, remove yourself from the situation, if possible, and prompt yourself to activate bilateral stimulation in your preferred mode immediately, before you get emotionally hijacked. Implementing this intervention can really be helpful in staying in the moment so you can decide how you would like to respond to the triggering event, and focus on the EMDR, rather than on how insulted, offended, or otherwise emotionally triggered you are. Focusing your attention on the bilateral stimulation can help you feel detached from the rage you were feeling when you were first triggered, and it can help you process your feelings and move forward, without damaging the situation further.

(IMPORTANT NOTE: Using any type of self-EMDR or bilateral stimulation is not recommended unless you have actually experienced EMDR with a licensed clinician who has been trained and certified as an EMDR practitioner. Ideally, your therapist can teach you the self-EMDR techniques, and be available to you should you encounter any difficulties or experience an unexpected reaction.)

Some other strategies also can help you to get into your left brain, and stay calm while processing what you are experiencing. A particularly effective technique is Mindfulness- Based Stress Reduction (MBSR), which teaches you to be "mindful in the face of fire," to practice mindfulness while being stressed by your narcissistic partner. MBSR has been shown in research to lower emotional and physiological measures of stress, and to help a person over time develop better coping mechanisms to deal with this sort of stress.

Meditation is another effective tool in calming the brain down by accessing the left brain. Purposeful, mindful concentration that allows you to find a peaceful place in your mind can take you away from the hot spots in the right brain and move you to the calmer environment of the left brain. Learning to meditate can help strengthen your ability to maintain control over how your brain responds to triggers without actually being emotionally triggered. It makes sense that if you become, with practice, able to get to a calm, peaceful place internally, it will be far less likely that the narcissist in your life can trigger you in a way that sends you emotionally out of control. Focus on creating a peaceful internal environment on a regular basis that makes being emotionally reactive less likely to occur, if not impossible.

Understanding Your Partner

To be effective in dealing with your narcissistic partner, it's critically important that you really understand him (or her)—how he became this way, what triggers him, and what his needs are. The more that you understand him in these important ways, the more likely you are to be able to anticipate sensitive areas and avoid triggering him. If you are focusing on meeting his legitimate needs and showing him how important it is to you to try to address them, you will be less likely to trigger the narcissism. If he feels loved, understood, and attended to, there is a better chance that he will give you the best of himself. If you make him feel judged, misunderstood, and neglected, you can be sure that you will get the narcissistic parts of him in their full glory.

To understand your partner, you first have to let go of the feelings of victimhood that you most probably are feeling and to work toward being other-centered and empathetic. Achieving more of a full understanding of who your partner is and why he became this way requires you to let go of yourself as the primary frame of reference and to focus more on him. This is not to say that you should enable him by not holding him accountable for his abusive behavior. Rather, it's more about keeping the focus on what he is feeling and needing, with the hope that, over time, your empathy will bring out the same in him. Empathy is also empowering, both in not allowing yourself to be in the role of the victim and in feeling the inner strength that comes with feeling real empathy for a damaged person.

Case Example 38: Paula and Raymond

As a seasoned, highly acclaimed teacher in a local public school, Paula was a bright, organized, and articulate woman in her late 40s. She fully understood the dynamics of positive reinforcement and of building up a child to fulfill his or her potential. Unfortunately, she was unable to apply those skills and attitude toward her husband, Raymond, who was the successful head of an international hospitality organization. Raymond was also the victim of an abusive and emotionally impoverished childhood home, with an alcoholic father, and a mother who was perennially depressed and self-absorbed. Although he somehow developed the perseverance and resilience to overcome these enormous obstacles in his earlier life, he nevertheless demonstrated the narcissistic personality traits that are so common in people with this type of upbringing, in which there was no one home to nurture or care for the children.

Consequently, Raymond was highly sensitive and easily triggered, and very critical of his wife, although she was quite competent in raising their children and ably managing her responsibilities at school. He also had a difficult time relating to and connecting with their sons, whom he often criticized for any type of shortcoming or mistake. This was despite the fact that they were, in fact, lovely boys who did their best at school and at home.

This was particularly difficult for Paula because she grew up with a mother who was quite similar to Raymond. Her difficult, critical mother was completely insensitive to Paula's needs or those of her siblings. As a result, Paula would often react strongly to Raymond's behavior toward their sons, or toward herself, for that matter. She felt the need to protect her boys and advocate for them in a way that she did not experience as a young person growing up in such an unsafe, hostile environment.

Raymond, of course, experienced her, in turn, as negative and critical, which brought him back to his years at his own home. He harbored much resentment toward her, as a result, especially since she was so obviously attentive and kind to their sons, and critical and inattentive to him. This led to his angry, narcissistic treatment of Paula and the boys, which only further perpetuated the cycle that continued to push the marriage into a downward spiral.

Paula came in for therapy because she was deeply unhappy in her marriage and strongly ambivalent about whether or not to divorce Raymond. On the one hand, she had no respect for her husband and was extremely uncomfortable around him. On the other, he provided the financial security that she felt the boys needed to actualize their considerable potential. It was equally important for her that they be raised in an intact family and not have to go through the trauma of a divorce.

After meeting once with Raymond, it became painfully obvious to me that Paula was perpetuating his narcissism through her rejecting behavior, and that the cycle could only be reversed once she made changes in her approach toward him. Being a highly intelligent and pragmatic person, Paula began to understand what she had to do to turn things around. She decided that she would stop all the negativity and show more respect, gratitude, and attentiveness toward Raymond, with the hope that it would elicit more positive behavior from him. She used the aforementioned tool of a picture of him as a sad boy to remind her what he went through as a child to bring out the empathy that she knew she would need to turn herself around. She also used self-EMDR when she became triggered. That helped her stay in the present and focus on her ultimate goals, instead of her negative feelings toward him.

To her surprise, within a week of her change in attitude, Raymond became softer and less critical toward the family, and they actually discovered that there were still things that they enjoyed about each other. Raymond felt more respected and safe with Paula, and she became more focused on the positive things that she had seen in him when they married. To this day, Paula continues to do a masterful job of focusing on the positive in their relationship and building him up as a husband and a father. She credits therapy for saving their marriage, and their family.

Keeping the Focus on the Goal

As a cognitive-behavioral therapist, for me, it's all about goals. When I first meet a patient, I try to elicit by the end of our first session what the person wants to accomplish or get out of therapy. If he or she can't conceptualize or articulate a goal, then the first goal becomes coming up with some goals to be accomplished. Without goals, therapy, at least in my mind, becomes an expensive waste of time. Having a warm, trusting relationship, providing a safe environment in which a patient knows that painful feelings can be expressed safely, and sharing encouraging words that offer hope to an otherwise hopeless patient are all important elements of a successful therapy experience, but they are just prerequisites to accomplishing a patient's goals. They aren't goals in themselves.

So, when a patient with a narcissistic partner comes in for help, it is vitally important to establish what he or she wants to accomplish. Does she want to end the relationship, find a way to make it work, or just figure out what she really wants to accomplish? All of these are valid goals, and it's really up to you, as the patient, to decide what you want to do with the situation. A therapist can help you process your feelings about the decision, present some options in terms of treatment approaches, and give you his or her best sense of the prognosis of your partner, or the relationship, but then it's really up to you to decide what you want to achieve as a result of therapy.

Once you have established your goals, it's important to stay focused on them, instead of allowing your emotions to derail you and take you down the wrong path. So, if it's your goal to keep your family intact and to not go through the trauma of a divorce, then that has to be foremost in your mind when you get triggered, when your partner slips and becomes abusive again, or when you are feeling particularly sorry for yourself for being in this difficult situation. No matter how long you or your partner are engaged in the therapy process, your partner will be imperfect, and his or her behavior will probably never be 100% to your liking. Focusing on your ultimate goal keeps you grounded and makes it more difficult for you to be triggered to the point of losing it, and setting back the relationship if has started to gain some traction as a result of therapy. It also helps you to become more emotionally regulated and internally stable, which is a very important goal in and of itself.

Getting Help

Finally, let me offer a word of advice from someone who has worked with narcissistic people for over 30 years. Get help. Don't try to do this alone. Narcissism is an extremely challenging personality disorder to deal with, and it can break the best of us. It is vital that you get a therapist of your own, someone to whom you can turn for support, guidance, direction, and yes, to be challenged when you become part of the problem. A good therapist can achieve the delicate balance between providing badly needed support, validation, and encouragement, but, at the same time, holding you accountable for what you are doing to contribute to or maintain the toxic dynamic of your relationship. It is rare that a relationship breakdown is 100% the fault of one partner, and the other partner is doing absolutely nothing wrong or has no room for improvement. As was the case of Paula, you may be reacting in ways that are very directly contributing to the relational dynamic, without any awareness on your part. Be open to that information, because it's actually good news—because if you are part of the problem, then you can be part of the solution!

Finding the right therapist can be a daunting task. The best referral source is someone you know who has seen a therapist that he or she thought was effective, especially in a similar situation. Asking your family physician which therapists he or she uses for marital issues such as this may also be a helpful path. Psychologytoday.com is a particularly useful resource. It has a comprehensive and detailed listing of therapists in your area, along with their areas of expertise, their credentials, and a narrative describing who they are as therapists. You can search for clinicians who have experience in narcissism, and then interview them, either in person or over the phone, to see if the relationship "clicks" or not.

Chemistry is important here, so pay attention to how your gut is feeling when you talk to the therapist. The ideal is to find someone with significant experience in marital therapy and a clear understanding of and experience treating narcissistic patients. You want someone who will not be afraid to challenge you if you are part of the problem (which is probably the case). Someone who can only validate you and support you so that you feel good about yourself or your therapy may not be the optimal choice here, especially if you have decided to try to make things work.

Finally, with the help of a good therapist, you can evaluate when the situation is just too severe and intransigent to accommodate real change, and decide to let it go. Not everyone can tolerate therapy, especially in the case of dealing with someone who has full-blown Narcissistic Personality Disorder. With the help of your therapist, you can decide, once it's been determined that your partner is really beyond help, to end the relationship, heal, rebuild yourself, and move forward.

With therapy, you can act with much more awareness and insight about how and why you got into a relationship with someone who is incapable of loving you and sustaining a real relationship, so that you can start over with someone who can. The bottom line is that if your present partner is just completely incapable of changing and transforming into a loving, respectful spouse, you deserve to be loved and respected, and you can achieve that goal—with someone else.

CHAPTER 20

Maintaining Your Integrity and Dignity: Balancing Loving and Setting Limits

Integrity and Dignity

Sustaining your integrity with a partner who lacks integrity, or maintaining your dignity when abusive, narcissistic behavior seems to rob you of it is often difficult. But, I think that it would be safe to say that a primary goal in dealing with a narcissistic partner is to maintain both your integrity and dignity, while trying to work effectively with him or her in respectfully setting limits.

What comes to mind when you think of integrity? In my mind, it involves being consistent and congruent over time with what you say and do, and being fair and accurate in what you communicate. It's also about being honest and moral in your interactions with the people in your life and society as a whole. That's not a standardized Webster's definition, but rather one that I've developed over a lifetime of working on my own integrity, as well as helping my patients work on theirs.

Dignity is a separate but, perhaps, related concept, that focuses more on the preservation of your self-respect, and earning, even requiring, the respect of others. Moreover, dignity involves self-control, purposeful behavior, and not allowing yourself to be lowered to the level of dysregulation of your emotions and behavior that your partner is exhibiting at a particular time. Dignity is about keeping your cool in the face of fire, establishing how you want to function in a difficult interpersonal interaction, and sticking to it. Also, perhaps more importantly, it's about being who you want to be, and presenting yourself the way you decide to show up in a challenging situation, despite attempts to knock you off center.

Maintaining your integrity and dignity in a relationship with a narcissistic partner can be very challenging, to say the least, especially if your partner is abusive to you. It often pushes you beyond your limits, and makes it quite difficult to stay calm and rational. However, if you stay consciously mindful about the goal of maintaining your integrity and dignity, there is a good chance that you can keep your cool, stay honest and real, and speak your truth. The goal is to make it impossible for your partner to bring you down to his or her level but, rather, for you to bring your partner up to your level of mature, respectful communication. That means that you have to use your own morals and standards of behavior as your reference point, instead of allowing his or her level of values and behavior to influence your reactions.

As I've mentioned repeatedly, this requires mindful awareness of what you are trying to accomplish in every interaction and, perhaps even more important, what you want to avoid at all costs. This mindfulness can keep you focused on your reference point and goals, and help you, once again, to be successful in maintaining your integrity and dignity.

Enabling Versus Aggression

Striking a balance between the extremes of being passive or enabling, and becoming aggressive or abusive when reacting to your partner's manipulation and abuse is often difficult to achieve while enduring the distress of this type of relationship. Mood swings and emotional instability are common experiences in a relationship with a narcissist, especially when he or she engages in "gaslighting."

This is a term that refers to narcissist's tendency to turn the focus to the partner's emotional reactions as the "real" problem and the root cause of the relationship difficulties. It's a fairly sophisticated attempt at projection, designed to manipulate you as the partner into believing that you and your reactions are really the problem, instead of the behavior that triggered the reactions in the first place. Gaslighting can cause either extreme of behavior. It can force a partner to become passive and submissive, as a result of the shame of being the cause of the relationship problems, or it can elicit rage as a result of the constant manipulation and shifting of the blame on to you.

Your goal is to prevent your partner from maneuvering you into constantly being the one at fault and triggering you to extreme behavior. You want to move the focus back to your partner calmly and skillfully and hold him or her responsible for the conflict that was caused by the narcissistic behavior. The key is to land in the middle of the extreme between being passive or aggressive, which is learning how to validate the narcissist's feelings, while also being assertive at the same time.

Effective Communication: Importance of Validation and Assertiveness

Effective communication is vital to the success and stability of all relationships, especially when you are dealing with someone with a narcissistic personality. So, what does "effective communication" mean? Within this context, I believe it refers to the middle ground between passivity and aggressiveness. So, instead of being overly submissive or deferential, you validate whatever you can to show your partner that you are open to hearing his or her point of view and to find areas of agreement or things that are being said that could be valid. By doing so, you set the example of taking the high road and, hopefully, you set the tone of the conversation so your partner will follow your lead. As has been previously mentioned, narcissists have a high need to be heard and validated, probably because they never experienced that while they were growing up. So, if you want to reach your partner emotionally, always start with some sort of validation, before making your own point.

Once you have done the validation, then you must be clear and assertive as to what you will and will not tolerate, in terms of the behavior that you experience in the relationship. Being assertive means clearly, but respectfully, expressing your feelings, needs, or opinions in a way that the other person is most likely to be able to hear. Consequently, he or she may also be more likely to respond to you in a more appropriate manner than if you were to be reactive or aggressive. Clear, effective communication also involves being specific as to what you expect to happen, or not happen, in future interactions, if the relationship is going to be sustained.

Assertiveness requires a strong core and, at the same time, it builds a strong core within you. It is self-reinforcing, in that the more that you practice and succeed in being assertive, the more likely you will want to continue to do so. Being assertive builds up your self-esteem and confidence. This should be the case regardless of how your partner responds or reacts to you. If, as hoped, he or she responds in a more appropriate, respectful way, then that surely will increase your confidence and inner strength. If that does happen, it is really important for you to take the opportunity to let your partner know that you noticed the change in attitude and to say how much you appreciate it. Positive reinforcement is always more effective than complaining and criticizing, especially when it is done with sincerity.

However, even if he or she continues to be aggressive or argumentative, you can keep your neutral stance, and know his or her behavior is really not your problem—but the narcissist's—so you can choose to disengage. You don't have to continue to be exposed to toxic behavior, and you always have the choice to calmly and respectfully inform your partner that you will not continue to engage with him or her under the present circumstances. However, if he or she wishes to try again in a more honest and respectful tone at a later time, perhaps when you are both calmer and in a more conducive frame of mind, you would be more than happy to reengage, but with the goal of mutual respect and resolving the conflict in a respectful manner.

Good Relationship Building Strategies

In Chapter 17, we reviewed several ways to improve your ability to be other-centered with your partner, resolve conflicts, and deepen the level of intimacy and connection in your relationship. Once again, using the MORE method, you can be more mindfully aware of your partner's baggage, feelings, and needs, as well as of the dynamic and pattern in your relationship that you wish to avoid. It also can prompt you to be other-centered and focus on what your partner is feeling or needing right now, as opposed to focusing only on your own feelings and needs. MORE also forces you to challenge negative thought patterns or judgmental conclusions about your partner and to reframe them into those that are more positive or fair-minded. And finally, it encourages you to work on being more empathetic toward your partner, by giving him or her the benefit of the doubt, as you remember what he or she went through as a child that shaped his or her personality in such a damaging way.

The RVRR method is an excellent tool for dealing with conflict and working on a mutually agreed upon resolution, instead of allowing arguments and conflicts to cause your relationship to deteriorate further. It focuses on the need to reflect back to your partner consciously what you heard and to sincerely validate what you can, so that he or she feels respected and can see that there is some common ground. It also sets the stage for you to respond with what you feel or need, with a greater probability that you will actually be heard. Finally and, perhaps, more importantly, it guides you both to focus on and work actively toward a successful resolution of the conflict, so that you both can put it behind you and move forward with a minimum of damage or residual resentment.

Finally, intensive weekend experiences such as Getting the Love You Want, provided by Harville Hendrix's Imago Therapy program, and Adventure in Intimacy with Hedy Schleifer, can open up lines of intimacy and teach you communication and relationship skills that can transport your relationship to new heights and levels of closeness that you could never have imagined. I strongly encourage you to sign up for one of these weekend seminars or to find another one that can strengthen your connection with your spouse and help you break through the barriers and defenses that have kept you from having a mutually satisfying relationship.

Remembering Your Contribution to the Relationship Problem, But…

Maintain a good balance between focusing on what your responsibilities are to make your relationship work, on the one hand, and not exclusively seeing yourself as the victim, and on the other hand, holding your partner accountable for taking responsibility to do what is needed to work on his or her awareness of the relevant personality issues and to develop the skills required to improve the relationship.

This balance is critical for you to maintain your emotional equilibrium and to allow you to keep a healthy perspective in which you don't take things too personally and absorb the negativity and criticism from your partner in a way that can damage you further. At the same time, be emotionally honest about acknowledging your own flaws (we all have faults—perhaps some more than others) and recognizing that being part of the problem is actually a good thing, because, if you are a part of the problem, you also can be part of the solution.

However, when all is said and done—

… Remember That It's Really Not All About You

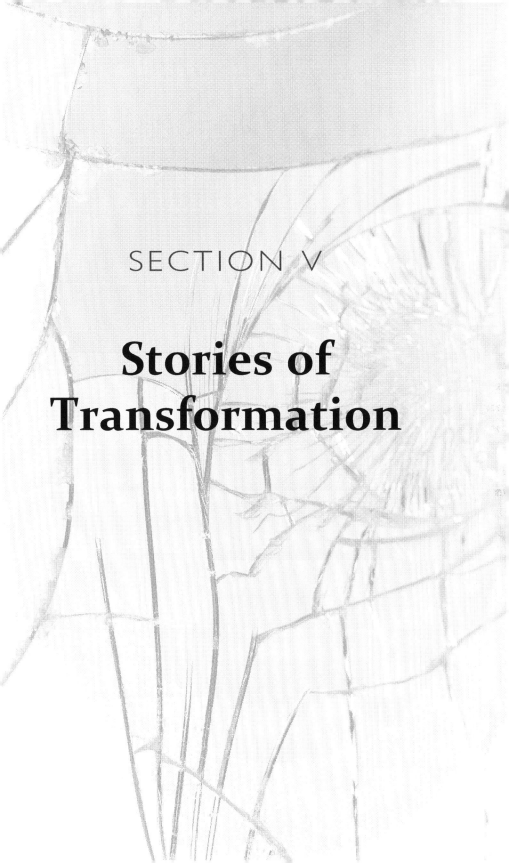

SECTION V

Stories of Transformation

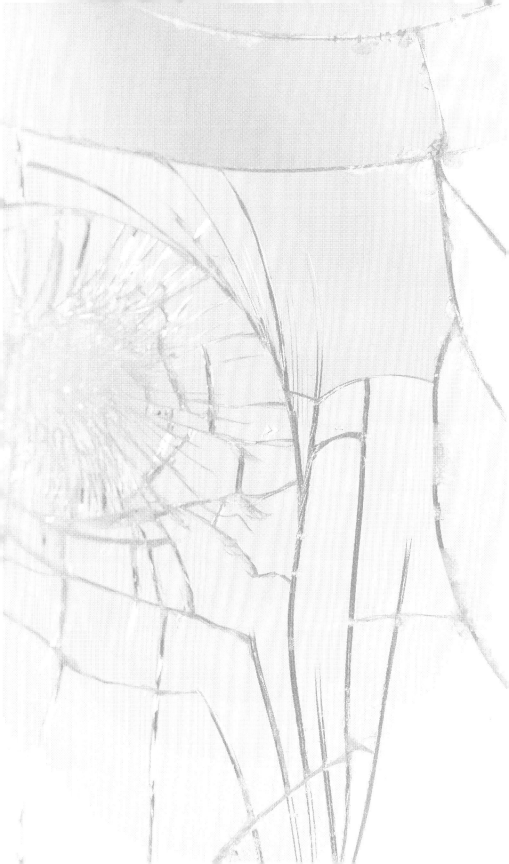

CHAPTER 21

Patients' Personal Stories: Inspirational Transformation

These patients have stories of transformation about their treatment for narcissism.

KENT

Narcissism recovery is a lifetime process. In my experience over the last four years, I have learned that narcissism recovery centers around my awareness of my own narcissistic tendencies and how they manifest themselves through my thoughts, actions, and feelings. Recovery from this condition is also about the acceptance that this is a personality trait that must be managed with diligence and compassion for both myself and the people that I impact. It is also a practice in persistence, since every day I face challenges that can disrupt my recovery.

Narcissistic traits have been a part of my personality and a default psychological protection mechanism for me since I was a young man. For me, I believe the root causes of these traits can be found in three main areas. First, I believe I have a possible genetic proclivity for certain narcissistic personality traits as demonstrated by other family members who also have these same strong narcissistic traits. Second, I grew up in an environment where these traits were modeled, in both my immediate and extended family. Third, I grew up in a home with a deprived social and emotional environment that I believe fostered narcissistic traits as a coping mechanism.

Prior to starting therapy and recovery, I viewed narcissism as an extreme form of vanity and egomaniacal behavior. I had no idea the range in which the various narcissistic personality traits could manifest themselves. I did not realize that narcissism included a range of traits and behaviors that I used to shield myself from psychological stress and pain. And while it may have shielded me from unpleasant feelings and situations, it also kept me emotionally distant, immature, and not present in my life. It was also a catalyst for addiction. Narcissism never really protected me and often prevented me from "feeling" the harm that my actions may have been inflicting on others or from truly feeling and, thereby, processing emotional situations.

Developing a personal core and the subsequent healing from that work has allowed me to significantly reduce the prevalence of narcissistic traits in my personality and life and has been the foundation for tremendous personal growth. However, it was not easy or comfortable to take down this "shield" that "protected" me, developed over years, and was a constant companion for decades. This has required a tremendous amount of work involving daily reflection and self-awareness.

However, I would never trade a life behind a mask of narcissism for a life full of the joys and challenges of living an emotionally available and present-focused life. My relationships with almost every person in my life have improved so significantly that it is terrifying to think of what my life would have been like had I not sought treatment or pursued it with earnestness and determination.

There is no free lunch. You get what you give. While narcissism is a dark and lonely space, there are options and a path out into the light. Humility, a stronger core and compassion for myself and others have been powerful antidotes. I have amends to make that will continue for my lifetime, but I am grateful to know myself enough that I can acknowledge my narcissism and work on it every day.

TOM

I am an only child of an immigrant, lower middle-class family. I excelled in school to become a successful professional, but I lacked the nurturing affection of a parent. I have learned that this created fertile grounds for narcissism with obsessive-compulsive behavior. These manifested in my early adulthood as an addictive pattern of sexual behaviors, which eventually led to the collapse of my integrity as a person.

In my early childhood, I was very involved in my religion of origin (Catholicism). My parents were not great believers or practicing Catholics, but I gravitated naturally to the faith of my grandparents. We immigrated during my middle school years to a country where I had to learn the language. In retrospect, that was not that easy, but I adapted rather well. My parents provided for me as well as they could financially for good schooling and some indulgences. They did the best they could with what they had, but they lacked emotional insight and ability.

I did well in school, and eventually went to graduate school to obtain a doctorate degree and married my high school sweetheart. In retrospect, I started lying to my wife the day I met her, when I told her I was in high school (rather than middle school) and didn't disclose to her I had another girlfriend while I was dating her. We married during my later years in college, and I went on for my doctorate degree followed by specialty training. We had three children while I was in school.

Life was good, but my pattern of obsessive and compulsive sexual behaviors began to emerge. I had affairs with other women, one lasting a rather long time, intermittently over several years. My philandering took me to the verge of divorce 30 years ago. Thanks to a psychologist whom I started seeing, I was able to save my marriage at least temporarily. Sex addiction was not on the radar of psychologists 30 years ago. I clearly behaved like a narcissist, but I was not diagnosed with a Narcissistic Personality Disorder and, I dare say, only overt pathological narcissists were diagnosed with "narcissistic personality."

By the grace of God, I was able to continue "functioning" in everyday life, but years after this episode, I returned to philandering again. Eight years ago, once again my indiscretions came to the attention of my wife and others. This time, she kicked me out of the house, and I reached a new "bottom." I sought psychological help, and my first therapist quickly identified that I had "sexual addiction." She guided me to Sex Addicts Anonymous (SAA), a 12-step program for recovery from sexual addiction. I started going to SAA meetings six or seven nights per week, got a sponsor, worked the steps, and saw my life starting to turn around. I made a commitment to myself to remain sexually sober whatever it took.

During my early recovery, I recognized that my spiritual bank was "bankrupt," that those values I held in early childhood were gone, and that my moral compass did not have a course. While I remained sober, and my wife had agreed "cautiously" to let me return home, I still had many secrets I had not disclosed to her. About two years into my recovery, my wife read my first step in SAA, which I had hidden very well. I had not disclosed many of the behaviors that I had written about and, thus, once again, I broke her trust. Under recommendation of one of my fellow SAA members, I started working with Dr. Goldwasser, a psychologist who specializes in sex addiction and narcissism.

My formal psychological evaluation confirmed that I had strong "narcissistic traits," so I had to tackle my addictive behavior and narcissism one day at a time. In addition to weekly therapy sessions with Dr. Goldwasser, I joined a group of his male patients who meet to share and obtain feedback from each other under his supervision. This group proved to be very beneficial with regards to listening to both success stories and miserable failures. Most importantly, this group provided a solid basis for its members to recognize and practice awareness of the manifestation of narcissistic traits.

The great acronym MORE (mindfully aware, other-centered, reframe, empathize), became my mantra when dealing with my wife and others. I continued therapy, group session (aka Fight Club) and SAA meetings. Things were going along well. I remained sober, worked with sponsors in the SAA group, and my home life was OK. One day my wife asked for "complete disclosure," and I was faced with a difficult decision. I agreed to it, and the disclosure occurred in Dr. G's office with his guidance (I don't recommend anyone giving full disclosure on his or her own without professional help). Toward the end of the disclosure session, my wife asked whether or not I was involved with anyone whom I had not told her about.

There was one person I had not planned on disclosing; however, under the urging of Dr. G, as well as sense of being driven by a strong moral force (God) and, without hesitation, I blurted out the name of the person. It was almost automatic, painful, and at the same time cathartic. This was once again devastating to my wife, since it was someone she knew very well. I don't know how she was able to pick up the pieces after this very shameful revelation. By the grace of God, and after a difficult few months, she was able to begin healing. She was engaged in her own therapy and Eye Movement Desensitization and Reprocessing (EMDR) therapy with Dr. G, as well as attending meetings of S-Anon (a 12-step program for the relatives and friends of sexually addicted people). Honesty is the cornerstone of recovery; without it, there remains a darkness that can cast a shadow on even many years of being sober.

Seven-plus years sober and in recovery, I now recognize that my philandering was medication for my inadequacies. I was trying to fill a hole in my heart left by the lack of a nurturing mother by endlessly seeking validation from women. My life in addiction revolved around a need for external validation. My lack of awareness was a set of blinders put on by my self-centeredness, which kept me clueless and in the dark and unable to connect the dots. Recovery radically changed this one day at a time. Validation now comes from the gentle caress of God in my life through his blessings, ever reminding me of His presence. I have found that cooperation and communication with God are necessary and vital to recovery. Recognizing my blessings, with gratitude, honesty and humility, removed the blinders of self-centeredness making me able to see more clearly and live and practice a virtuous life.

Three years into my recovery, my mother died of cancer. I will never forget the day before her death. I stood by her bedside and asked her if she prayed. She said, "Not as much as you do." I began praying with her, and the next day she died. I won't forget those words. She validated several things for me: My spiritual life was very evident to those around me, in particular, my parents, wife and children. Praying and consciously practicing meditation every day form the basis of my recovery. God speaks to me daily through people, places, things, situations, and scriptures. And finally, to listen, I have to be aware, and have an open heart and mind, and be attentive to Him.

I am still married, by the grace of God. I continue to work on myself through the SAA program, by attending meetings, sponsoring others, and volunteering countless hours at my local church. I am amazed how God has worked in my life. My relationship with my wife continues to improve, though it has its ups and downs, certainly more ups than downs. My relationship with my oldest son (who witnessed one of my philandering episodes when he was young) has also significantly improved. As for myself, I am a "work in progress."

MARCOS

I was born to a narcissist father who, like his mother, married an enabling partner. Yet, my childhood memories were pleasant for the most part. My immigrant parents struggled and worked hard so that my siblings and I never lacked anything. Our parents were loving, giving, and nurturing. It wasn't until my pre-teen years that I felt something was off. My father was an overbearing, critical disciplinarian. This created a sense that I was not good enough and left me with low self-esteem. I felt less than my friends, my brother, and especially my father.

He was an imposing man, a force to be reckoned with who sucked the oxygen out of a room. At home, he yelled and intimidated us to maintain order. Corporal punishment was a staple for my siblings and me, until one day, he stopped after a scare with my brother.

I could sense when something was about to happen and would often hide in my room to avoid being caught in the fray. After every "event,"

I distinctly remember having thoughts of running away or committing suicide.

As an early teen I medicated my pain with porn and masturbation, lying and embellishing to prop up my low self-esteem. I developed a sense of entitlement, emulating my Dad's ways of dealing with life. It all seemed normal, after all Dad was very successful financially and in his married life, and I aspired to be like him.

Soon after graduating from college, I met the love of my life. We got married and had three beautiful children. Financial pressures with my business as well as old sibling rivalry issues with my brother, who was my business partner, brought out the narcissistic traits I learned growing up. But my behavior was normal, or so I thought.

I went through explosive outbursts of yelling and screaming at my wife and kids followed by shutting down verbally, isolating myself, and playing the victim, but that was all normal for me. I did not confront my narcissistic traits until years later when my wife discovered my addiction to porn, and I started therapy.

I know now that the way I behaved was based on entitlement and distorted reality. I was emotionally abusive toward my wife and kids. My behavior caused emotional trauma and psychological damage to those I love. My guilt and shame were painful and, at times, overwhelming, which made my road to recovery difficult and long. Confronting the demons of my childhood and taking responsibility for my life through therapy enabled me to make amends with those I had hurt, including myself.

Therapy and a spiritual program were the key. I learned how to see the world through the eyes of other people by putting myself in their shoes and developing empathy. It was as if I had been carrying around a 200-pound backpack full of rocks my entire life. As I started to work on myself, the pack got lighter and lighter. I finally felt good about who I truly am. My self-esteem became stronger and the dark clouds dissipated.

Today my marriage is stronger than ever, my relationships with my children are loving and healthy, and I feel peace, serenity and happiness. I am truly blessed.

EARL

Therapy has made a significant impact on my life. I was introduced to my psychologist during a period of great personal crisis. My marriage was falling apart, and I felt like my world was being rocked at the very core. I turned to a trusted friend for guidance, and he strongly encouraged me to meet with Dr. Goldwasser. At the onset, he proved to be a voice of reason and calm.

Through therapy, I was able to understand that I would be able to get through this challenge, and that I was being presented with an opportunity to achieve massive personal growth if I was willing to put in the work. I am very grateful that this turned out to be true.

Prior to working with Dr. Goldwasser, I was quite indifferent, even resistant, to the concept of therapy. I felt that it could be helpful for those who sought it, but I never viewed myself as one who really needed it. My life had played out in a manner that largely exceeded my expectations going into 2014.

I was 39 at that time. I believed that hard work, dedication, and resilience were the aspects of my personality that had allowed me to enjoy success in the endeavors that were important to me. I felt that I was generally well-liked by others and was fortunate to enjoy very rewarding friendships. I would soon learn that my view of myself was accurate on some levels, but I was completely unaware of another dimension of my personality.

In our initial meetings together, we took a close look at my past and present. Dr. G. asked insightful questions, and he listened intently to the story of my life. It became quite clear early on that I carried some scars from experiences that I had encountered as a child. I had never really processed how some of my early challenges could have affected me in a negative way. I always believed that overcoming the obstacles in my path made me stronger.

Therapy helped me see my life more fully and objectively. For the first time, I was able to identify and accept that I had a narcissistic personality. I was generally well intentioned in how I pursued my life, but

I had an utter lack of self-awareness. I was clueless as to how I really affected others and was completely void of empathy. I could see life only through my own lens and generally believed that my views were right all of the time. Furthermore, I was unable to recognize or accept any of my personal weaknesses or take responsibility for my mistakes. I had deep rooted insecurities that manifested when I pointed out how great I was on any number of other fronts whenever I was confronted with criticism, whether perceived or real. In short, it was all about me, all of the time. I was constantly in my own head, telling myself a narrative that was highly flawed. Unsurprisingly, these qualities affected relationships that I cared deeply about in a highly negative fashion, and I lacked the emotional attunement to get it, at all.

Today I am grateful that I am able to experience life with a much higher degree of awareness. Therapy helped me resolve the inner conflicts that prevented me from feeling inner peace. The anger and resentments over my past are not part of my present, and my life is incredibly more enjoyable as a result. Through my work in therapy, I developed the skill of being "other-centered." I consciously endeavor to understand the perspective and feelings of other people. I strive to consider how my words and actions will affect those around me. These attributes have allowed me to be far more effective in my personal relationships. I presently operate at a much higher level as a father, son, brother, and friend; these are my highest priorities in life.

In addition, I have observed many instances in my business where I have benefited directly from the progress that I have made over the years in therapy. It has also been very gratifying for me to receive positive feedback from family members, friends, and business associates whom I have known for many years for the changes that they observe within me. I have been told that I am more thoughtful, caring, a better listener, and less self-aggrandizing. People also sense that I am calmer and appear to be at peace with myself.

I have experienced the personal growth and positive evolution that Dr. G indicated was possible at the beginning of this process if I were willing to work on myself. I now regularly turn to him for guidance and support as I endeavor to be my best and live a full and rewarding life. I am deeply grateful to him for his professionalism, wisdom, and care. I fully believe that the best is yet to come for me. I was once asleep; I am now awake.

JOCELYN

I first came to see Dr. G many years ago to work on my marriage with my then-husband, who was, I thought, the real cause of all my problems. He was hard to live with and limited. He undermined me with our children and our business, and he was basically a poor excuse for a husband. My sole focus was on how tortured I was and what a victim I was of his behavior and his difficult personality.

After many frustrating and fruitless efforts in therapy, and a lot of soul-searching, I finally decided to divorce him. The divorce was even more torturous than our marriage, but finally we were able to end it once and for all, and I was able to start my new life. I was finally rid of the nemesis who had plagued me all those years.

The next few years were a rude awakening because many of the problems that I had experienced in my life seemed to persist, despite the fact that my husband was no longer there to torment me. I still seemed to be having problems with my kids, the people in my business, and even my friends and family members. Suddenly, I realized, with the help of therapy, that maybe I was also part of the problem, and that my own personality was getting in the way of having the kind of relationships that I wanted to have, especially with my kids. As therapy proceeded, and my kids gave me more honest feedback about how they found me to be difficult, as well, I realized that I needed to start taking a good long look at my own "stuff." I had to learn to modify my behavior and my reactions in a way that would make my relationships work, instead of creating more drama for myself and the people I love.

It wasn't always easy, trust me. There were days when I walked out of Dr. G's office swearing I would never come back again, because he just didn't "get it." Often when he would challenge me, I felt betrayed; I even felt I needed to get a new therapist. But over time, I started to realize that he was right and, as he would say often, "The good news is that you're part of the problem, because now you can become part of the solution."

I started to really take in what he was saying, and I tried to look at things from the perspective of the other people in my life. I tried to be less judgmental and to have some empathy for their struggles, especially my kids, who went through such difficult times having such a dysfunctional family. Instead of acting defensive and angry, I tried to listen more to my relatives when they tried to give me feedback about how I was dealing with things. I began getting feedback from friends that they were starting to see me soften up. They saw that I was becoming less harsh and reactive, and they hoped I would continue with whatever I was doing that was causing these changes. I didn't have the inner strength to let them know that I was in therapy, because I was afraid to show my vulnerabilities and my deficiencies.

However, over time, I started to share what I was doing with people close to me, and the response was overwhelming. They were so proud of me that I had started to take matters into my own hands, and—instead of being the victim all the time—to take responsibility for the problems that I often caused due to my own behavior and personality issues. The feedback felt so good; the truth is, I never got compliments from my parents, who were very harsh and judgmental in their own right. I was never built up or made to feel special or good about myself. Finally, with the changes that I was making, my children became more responsive and warmer to me, my friends were showering me with positive feedback, and my family members started to interact with me more and invited me more to family functions. It was really a transformational experience for me. I really cherish and appreciate my personal change, and I'm grateful for what it has done for my life and my family.

It wasn't easy facing the fact that I had a narcissistic personality, and I know I still have traits that come up from time to time. However, therapy has liberated me from all of the pain and anguish I experienced being the victim of my own behavior and bringing out the worst in people around me. Now that I've learned to bring out the best in them, they are responding in ways that seem to bring out the best in me. I feel that I have a real chance of having some happiness in my life, perhaps for the first time, and I have to tell you it feels awfully good.

For those who are struggling with these types of problems, please know that there is hope for you. There are solutions and real opportunities in therapy to make changes that are necessary to turn your life around and to make all of your relationships work better. Don't be afraid to give it a try because you'll never regret it!

About the Author

Dr. Norman Goldwasser is a clinical psychologist and Director of Horizon Psychological Services in Miami Beach, Florida, for over 30 years. He is an internationally known clinician, and has been a featured speaker on a wide range of topics in South Africa, Australia, Hong Kong, Israel, and throughout North America.

He specializes in the treatment of trauma, addictions, marital conflict, sexual abuse, and identity issues. Most important, he is the proud grandfather of 23 grandchildren spread across the U.S. and Israel!

Made in United States
Orlando, FL
10 November 2023

38799813R00135